INSCRUTABLE EATING

INTERSECTIONAL RHETORICS
Karma R. Chávez, Series Editor

INSCRUTABLE EATING

ASIAN APPETITES AND THE RHETORICS OF RACIAL CONSUMPTION

Jennifer Lin LeMesurier

THE OHIO STATE UNIVERSITY PRESS

COLUMBUS

Published by The Ohio State University Press.

Library of Congress Cataloging-in-Publication data available online at https://catalog.loc.
gov
LCCN: 2022045095
Identifiers: ISBN 978-0-8142-1537-1 (cloth); ISBN 978-0-8142-5867-5 (paper); ISBN 978-0-
8142-8281-6 (ebook)

Cover design by Alexa Love
Text composition by Stuart Rodriguez
Type set in Minion Pro

♾ The paper used in this publication meets the minimum requirements of the American
National Standard for Information Sciences—Permanence of Paper for Printed Library
Materials. ANSI Z39.48-1992.

CONTENTS

ILLUSTRATIONS

Orienting toward Race at the Table

In my undergraduate years, I was a good student in that I knew how to strategically take classes that fed my particular set of strengths while never threatening the GPA standard I had set for myself (every professor's dream). One quarter, this meant that instead of taking the notorious weed-out Intro to Biology course, I enrolled myself in an Intro to Fishery Sciences course that promised some interesting readings about fish without the pesky tests on the different parts of a cell. The class itself was good and impactful (I still curate my fish intake according to the MSC Fisheries Standard), but I mostly remember it now for an incident that occurred outside of the class. Like many intro classes, you either came in with a friend group, or you found the other singles and duos who were palatable to talk to during small discussions. I frequently found myself sitting next to a fellow sophomore, a white girl who was quiet but nice. As my consciousness of what it meant to be a high-achieving Asian American girl in a West Coast environment was not fully fleshed out until grad school, I literally thought nothing of our different racial identifications until one day post-class.

She asked me what I was doing for lunch. I replied that I had brought an instant noodle bowl, and I joked about how it was the kind with far too much sodium and yet too little flavor. She responded, "Oh, so you're going to stink up the place like one of 'those' Asians?" with a small smile.

As we said our goodbyes, I thought the comment was a bit rude but otherwise moved on with my day. I grew up on the West Coast, adopted into a white family with a fellow adopted sister (who everyone swore looked just like me even though she was born in Vietnam and I in South Korea), which meant the noodle bowl was as exotic a food to me as it was to my classmate. It was only much later when I realized that my classmate framing her statement as a joke that we should both be able to share was made possible through a belief in the natural alignment of racial embodiment and certain ways of eating.

This fleeting moment points to some of the warrants that underpin how race, food practices, and associated embodiments are made to cohere in everyday rhetorical messaging. My classmate was speaking of a broad stereotype—Asian food is smelly—but what is more interesting are the assumptions that supported her using this stereotype in a joke that she thought would be amusing to an Asian American classmate. There were evidently aspects of my behavior that I can only guess that made this classmate feel as though I would respond favorably to a cordoning off of "those" Asians: speaking English with no accent, white boyfriend, no other Asian friends in that class, willingness to ask questions in a crowded lecture hall, etc. . . . Regardless, her comment demonstrates the power of eating practices to supersede other racial markers.

In *Inscrutable Eating,* I propose that the rhetorical formation of categories like race, gender, sexuality, and class are inextricable from rhetorics of exclusion based on fictitious, opposing embodiments of queerness and normalcy, exemplified by how the body chooses, or supposedly chooses, to eat. Specifically, because eating is a vulnerable process whereby one keeps "the orifices of the body open," ways of eating are overladen with beliefs about the right and wrong way to inhabit a body and perform its identities.[1] The supposed binary between eating as a pathway to moral superiority versus falling victim to all sorts of bodily ills is part of the same epistemological grounding that motivates fears about miscegenation, sexual deviance, and gender performance. When these moral hierarchies become attached to food, an object that is often used to emphasize the personal, as in "personal taste," these segregating measures can be posed as individual choices rather than investigated as tacit discriminatory vernaculars. The rhetorics that surround eating are a prime site "for the representation of, and fascination with, those bodies that carry the burdens of difference and materiality, that are understood as less social, less intellectual, and at times, less sentient."[2] So, a rhetorical follow-up to "You are what you eat" might be the simple question of "Says who?"

---

1. Ahmed, *Cultural Politics,* 83.
2. Tompkins, *Racial Indigestion,* 8.

In order to redress these gaps in our understanding of how food-related discourses enable certain hierarchies, I marry rhetorical analysis with essential scholarship in Asian American studies, cultural studies, history, and literature that centers identity formation and cultural representation. I do so to better understand what is so rhetorically appealing about the "benign culinary symmetries in which culinary tastes isomorphically align with bodies."[3] To clarify how these beliefs about bodies-that-eat elevate certain rhetorical possibilities over others, I pose and explore the following questions. What is the "sense-making" that people do in order to maintain boundaries between cuisines in their thinking, speaking, and eating practices? How do these sensory modes of evidence draw on and reinforce, or perhaps reflect, broader discursive and material structures of racism? Where is this boundary policing and diminishing about the food itself, taste in the most ordinary way, and where is it about broader senses of social contamination and purity? Which groups are expected to continually perform their cultural identity for the consumption of others, and how do such expectations reveal tacit attitudes about hierarchies of class, race, and gender? In exploring such questions, I clarify how inequities of attention and resources are enabled through gut orientations that center an oppositional relationship between disgust and desire. The rhetorical figuring of certain proximities to food and eaters as either loathsome or craveable maintains racialized spatiality under the guise of moral eating practices.

In the following chapters, I examine how Asian ontologies become welded to presumedly unhealthy and immoral eating practices through the embedding of biases related to class, gender, race, and sexuality in prominent rhetorics around food. What is consistent in the examples I pursue, from historical texts from the 1800s to contemporary examples from the twenty-first century, is the hyperbolic Othering of the Asian-as-ravenous-eater. However, there is also often an awareness of the pleasures of "eating the Other."[4] This oppositional binary of desire/disgust underpins rhetorical acts of exclusion that operate based on racist assumptions about appropriate embodiments and proximities. I investigate how these texts capture affective arcs related to ideas of Asian eating, "both as the pressure points of events or banalities suffered and the trajectories that forces might take if they were to go unchecked."[5] The expectations for performance of racial clarity are enacted and reenacted around food, embedding racial stereotypes not just in the surrounding discourses but also in the attendant feelings and affects.

In chapter 1, I open by defining "gut orientations" as the aggregate rhetorical force of discourses, feelings, and practices that reify unease/novelty in the

---

3. Mannur, *Culinary Fictions*, 7.
4. hooks, "Eating the Other."
5. Stewart, *Ordinary Affects*, 2.

presence of an Other's food and therefore tacitly support normative interracial proximities as a reflection of natural laws, rather than cultural biases. If one is guided uncritically by these gut orientations, the resulting forms of rhetorical interaction with eaters tend to reinforce dominant expectations for gender, race, sexuality, and the inequities fostered by such hierarchies. Through this exploration, I intervene in conversations on rhetoric and materiality by demonstrating how affect and sensation can be shunted into supporting stereotypes about racial and gendered embodiment. Although scholarship on emotion and embodiment demonstrates the intellectual paucity of definitions of rhetoric that elevate rationality above all else, attention to these arenas also requires awareness of how habituated feeling, especially when attached to commonsense definitions of intuition and taste, can become used in service of ideological commitments that do material harm.

In chapter 2, I analyze how the common metonymical link drawn between Asian male laborers and rats in the late 1800s was part of a broader conception of Asian male embodiment as forever beyond the reach of US morality because of their lack of heteronormative instincts. As consumption of luxury foods, like beef, became a key element of performing white masculinity, accusing Asians of consuming rats or in rat-like ways provided a focal point for broader suspicions of Asian familial structure, reproduction, and sexuality. I analyze popular folk texts and songs from this era alongside the notable anti-Chinese pamphlet "Some Reasons for Chinese Exclusion. Meat vs. Rice. American Manhood against Asiatic Coolieism. Which Shall Survive?" written by labor leaders Samuel Gompers and Herman Gutstadt. Collectively, these texts pose Asian male embodiment as a deviant, inscrutable gut that weakens labor forces, familial unity, and citizenship and must be expelled from US shores.

Chapter 3 returns to the figure of the Oriental rodent in the twenty-first-century furor over the coronavirus pandemic and the ensuing anti-Asian sentiment and violence. The fixation on the Chinese as "bat eaters" and thus an automatic source of the coronavirus grows out of the same rhetorical framing of Asian embodiment as that which threatens Western imperial power via queerly submissive allure. More specifically, long-standing fears of Asian feminine hypersexuality underpin contemporary fears of Asiatic eating, both stemming from beliefs that the Asian mouth is excessive in its prompting of unthinking orality. The initial furor and fear about "wet markets" and bat eating emerges from a dominant gut orientation that understands Asians as rapacious conflators of food and sex, exemplified by the tendency toward "queer licking."[6] Eating as an Asian is to be a dangerously queer character that flirts

6. M. Chen, *Animacies*, 185.

with the bestial, and the US must be proactive in warding off this deviant allure. To make this point, I analyze both how the fears about coronavirus descend from the original fears of the inscrutable immigrant and how they are still made manifest. The linkage of fears of consumption with fears of sexual deviance illustrates how the Asian body is still that which is too animal, too irrational, and too sensual to be fully admitted into a Western civic sphere.

Even when such fears are left tacit, they still render Asian food as that which always exceeds norms for eating in potentially harmful ways. In chapter 4, I examine the implicit whiteness of health and wellness discourse, particularly in relation to nutrition, to clarify how bodily feelings are centered as a nonracial metric for measuring contact with food. The bias against sensation sets up implicit food hierarchies, rather than overt racist violence; the animated embodiment of Asian food is always set in direct opposition to that of healthy, nonethnic food, tacitly reasserting Asianness as a lower-class, lower-quality contaminant that threatens to negatively alter the substance of the white body. In looking for these warrants of concern in the conversations around MSG and the opening of Chinese American restaurants by non-Chinese owners, we see how evidence of the overstimulated body is used as a way to place blame on Asian food and build the ethos of the non-Asian restauranteur, maintaining an oppositional orientation toward Asian epistemologies as normative. Food should be that which restores and soothes, not that which stimulates.

I turn to the supposedly more positive stereotype of the "model minority" in chapter 5 and explore how this archetype brackets Asian embodiment as that which still needs to be made palatable to white taste and racial discourse. To unpack some of these contradictions, I analyze a prominent *New York Times* article written by cultural critic Bonnie Tsui about the stereotypes used to talk about Asian food and its backlash. In the response to her article on stereotypical naming practices for Asian salads, Tsui's concern over stereotyping was rhetorically positioned as an affective transgression of sensitivity and obsession with authenticity. The expectations for discourse about Asian food to be race-neutral mirrors the expectations for Asians to be passive and docile "model minorities," expectations that view mention of Asian ethnic particularity as set against American values of multiculturalism and diversity. While direct accusations of queer eating might not be present, such beliefs hover in the background, ready to be used as rhetorical bludgeons against an Asian speaker that dares to exceed the expected feminized, passive stance.

I conclude with a brief discussion of what these cases demonstrate about the formation of race in the US. I argue we need to more deeply consider how gut orientations are a key part of the rhetorical framing of race relations. This examination of the intertwining of health, eating, and appropriate embodiment demonstrates the need to weigh seemingly commonsense "gut" reactions in our discussions about the rhetorical racial landscape and how future work on dismantling biased and/or racist rhetoric should attend to this felt sense of prejudice that underpins dominant orientations toward those deemed Other.

A NOTE ON NOMENCLATURE

A key rhetorical issue that I aim to substantively address in my investigation of stereotypes and experiences with Asian food is how the commonplaces embedded in the use of the term "Asian American" perpetuate an amalgamation of vaguely East Asian characteristics as Asian, essentially erasing the concerns of other Asian ethnicities from mainstream discourse. Originally, the term was coined in service of political unification alongside other civil rights movements in the 1960s, as an alternative to the outdated term "Oriental."[7] The category, although politically necessary when originated, is now burdened with simultaneously representing those "born in the United States and born in Asia, of exclusively Asian parents and of mixed race, urban and rural, refugee and nonrefugee, fluent in English and non-English speaking, professionally trained and working-class."[8] Several cultural and political events have aligned this category in the public eye with East Asian aesthetics and cultures. Due in large part to the influx of Chinese workers in the 1800s discussed in chapter 2, Chinese restaurants are the longest established and remain the most numerous of all Asian ethnic businesses (for comparison, the popularity of Thai restaurants in the US was only recently jump-started due to a Thai government cultural outreach program in the early 2000s). In 1972, President Nixon famously went to China and was filmed eating a feast of ornate foods, visiting landmarks like the Great Wall, and speaking with Chairman Mao in person. The twenty-first-century fascination with anime and K-Pop means that East Asian cultural aesthetics dominate. The rendering of Asia as coequal with just a few countries is especially evident in the wave of anti-Asian hate post-COVID where Asian victims, regardless of their actual geographic origin, are consistently told some version of "Go back to China."[9] Yet, as was demonstrated in the 2020 controversy over whether or not to label Vice President Kamala Harris as Asian American, biracial or non–East Asian identities

---

7. Zia, *Asian American Dreams.*

8. Lowe, *Immigrant Acts,* 66.

9. During the initial wave of racism against Asian Americans due to COVID-19, James Tang tweeted, "My mom said we should speak Thai in public so we don't get targeted for speaking Mandarin and I think it's so sweet that she's nice enough to believe that these stupid fucking racists can differentiate between Asian languages" (May 14, 2020).

often are not felt to fit in this category. The texts I am analyzing, while not representative of demographic realities, *are* representative of the usually unchallenged, tacit chain of reasoning that poses contact with Asian food and Asian people as one and the same.[10]

Because of these still-present ambiguities and conflations inherent in the term *Asian American,* I will purposefully use the broader term *Asian,* except when referring to rhetorics that focus on specific ethnic or community groups, in order to highlight how the dominant gut orientation toward Asianness centers an abstracted Asian embodiment, rather than a more particular ethnic or regional understanding. For the purposes of this project, I emphasize how the overarching gut orientation toward Asianness in the US is one that denies the presence of "American" within all such Asian bodies. Forefronting the racial category throughout will help illuminate how the projected normalizing force of the label of citizen, the "American" in "Asian American" or "Mexican American," does not supersede the still-dominant rhetorical assumption of danger embedded in more melanated bodies. The term "American" can distract from how the underlying gut orientation toward Asian bodies is still one that fears treachery and harm. Such attitudes are not separable from current rhetorical practices of speaking, writing, or listening, which means that Asian rhetors must build rhetorical credibility and legibility with an awareness, or perhaps even incorporation, of stereotypical expectations.

There are, of course, nuances of racism and exclusion that are particular to certain demographics: second-generation Asian Americans who hold US citizenship from birth and reside in the US, Asian expats from other countries who now hold US citizenship or green card status, biracial people who are deeply connected (or not) to the heritage of their parents, transracial adoptees, and so on. I anticipate the concept of gut orientations being useful in probing the term/imagined community of Asian Americans, or any "X American" community, to get at the nuance of subcategories and more closely parse how the cipher of "Asianness" or "X-ness" impacts the scope of perceived and taken rhetorical options.

---

10. Debates over what language to use for Asians in the US reflect this ongoing tension. For example, many argue that hyphenating "Asian-American" frames racial identity as a ratio from an unquestioned, centralized Americanness, especially given the acceptance of no hyphen in "African American" (personal email from Christina Fa Mark, Jan. 18, 2020). See also David Palumbo-Liu's discussion of his use of the solidus in "Asian/American" in *Asian/American: Historical Crossings of a Racial Frontier.*

ACKNOWLEDGMENTS

In working through the visceral, affective swirls of rhetorical force that coalesce in who we are and what we enact, I come face-to-face with the innumerable encounters and people who made this book not only possible but thinkable.

I am indebted to my mentors at the University of Washington and their ongoing encouragement to understand how rhetoric moves us and how movement is rhetorical. Anis Bawarshi, Candice Rai, and Gail Stygall have been unwavering in their support of my intellectual growth. Perhaps more importantly, they have all intervened in my life in ways that required extra effort on their part but that increased my capacity to care for others. I have told multiple people this, but it is worth repeating: I would not be the writer I am now without Candice's ever-patient guidance. One of my greatest aims is to follow her care-forward example as a teacher and researcher.

I owe great thanks to my colleagues in Writing and Rhetoric at Colgate University, past and present—Kermit Campbell, Cynthia Fields, Jenn Lutman, Jason Markins, Rob Mills, Ritika Popli, Tyler Rife, Ryan Solomon, Jeff Spires, Suzanne Spring, Meg Varney, Noah Wasan, and Meg Worley. Thank you for the many doorway conversations, detailed feedback on drafts, and rich engagement with my ideas. Many thanks also go to Colgate University's Faculty Research Council for their support of this project.

Numerous peers and mentors have read portions of this work, discussed all things food with me, or sustained my intellectual journey. Betsy Cooper is a force to be reckoned with, both in the dance studio and as a writing teacher. Rachel Arteaga, Alissa Bourbonnais, Rachel Kunert-Graf, Heather Hill, Maya Smorodinsky, and Lauren Summers Reinhardt gave me grace and love. The JEAN writing group supported me through several brain blocks and helped me approach my analysis with fresh eyes; many thanks to Stephanie Kerschbaum, Elisabeth Miller, Annika Konrad, Neil Simpkins, and Melissa Yang. Thank you to Nathan Johnson for talking all things soup and race with me and Will Penman for your modeling of caring pedagogy. Thanks to Aaron Wolf for getting me to see how I might approach such a book and Ashley Taylor for sending me all the links. Cheers to Boram Jeong, Greg Seigworth, Chad Shomura, and Michael Richardson for horizontal mentoring and fun at the Affect Theory conferences. And I deeply appreciate everyone at the Pewter Spoon who kept me fed and caffeinated as I wrestled with writing about food and consumption.

So many rhetorical scholars have helped me get to the level as a writer and thinker where I could write this book: Vanessa Beasley, Lillian Campbell, Steven Corbett, Dan Cryer, Kendall Gerdes, Drake Gossi, Scott Graham, Debra Hawhee, Jason Kalin, Michelle LaFrance, Timothy Oleksiak, Lester Olson, Damien Pfister, Nadya Pittendrigh, Kendall Phillips, Ryan Skinnell, Christa Teston, Anjali Vats, Myra Washington, Sharon Yam, and many more. My special thanks to the Reading Group and the joys of poring over theoretical tangles shared with John Ackerman, Christopher Ingraham, Bridie McGreavy, Candice Rai, and Nathan Stormer.

The labor and generosity of my peer reviewers transformed the scope and refinement of this book. I am ever grateful. Thanks also to the forward-thinking work of both Taralee Cyphers and Karma Chávez on expanding the scope and impact of rhetorical scholarship.

Nathan, I would not be here without you. Or I might, but the version of myself would be attenuated, less able to use what I do to give to others and work on the world around me. Love, love, love to you.

CHAPTER 1

Gut Orientations

"We speak ourselves, just as the food we eat is us. And, in the same way, the food speaks for us as well."[1] Raymie McKerrow makes this claim as part of a broader reflection on the contradictions inherent in his own personal history as a farm boy and his current dietary practices. On the one hand, he recognizes the deep connection between what we eat and the persona we project into the world, but on the other, his current inability to digest, and thus eat, wheat because of his Celiac disease is at direct odds with his upbringing on a wheat farm.[2] His embodiment of this seeming contradiction unsettles the common paraphrase of Jean Anthelme Brillat-Savarin's famous quote "Tell me what you eat and I'll tell you what you are" by modeling how this expectation quickly breaks down when attending to the physical body and its contexts.

Any telling of what we eat is more than a mere factual statement. Rather, such rhetoric organizes our relationships with food practices and creators in how it elevates certain ideological stances toward the material world as both expected and superior. Given that food, discourse, and materiality are deeply intertwined with issues of social and economic power, it is worth unpacking how food-related narratives intersect with broader assumptions of what

---

1. McKerrow, foreword, xii.

2. Kyla Wazana Tompkins's work in *Racial Indigestion* on Sylvester Graham's efforts at food reform demonstrates how wheat, through the figure of bread, played a key role in positioning the young United States as a "civilized" country.

one's place in the globally interconnected world should look like.[3] Particularly because the discourses surrounding eating and consumption are so often marked by identity markers such as race, ethnicity, and geography, to "be what you eat" is to have to negotiate the tension between one's cultural consumption practices and the biases held about those practices embedded in mainstream discourse. These biases are both spoken and felt; common ways of discussing consumption *orient* our ways of speaking and eating away from certain practices and therefore toward or away from certain racial characteristics. More specifically, these rhetorics of consumption enable particular *gut orientations* toward and away from certain communities through the medium of food practices that are moralized as either "good" and clean or "bad" and dirty.

In her discussion of the phenomenology of orientation, Sara Ahmed describes how the foregrounding and backgrounding of attention to arrangements of bodies and objects normalize where bodies belong in relation to others and other objects. "Some things are relegated to the background to sustain a certain direction, in other words, to keep attention on the what that is faced. Perception involves such acts of relegation that are forgotten in the very preoccupation with what it is that we face."[4] In thinking about rhetorics of consumption, whether of food, politics, or luxury goods, the entrainment of recognition operates within the encountering body as the urge to taste further or to recoil. These culturally dominant understandings of what is good and bad to eat maintain specific, preset bodily proximities between races as natural and mark alternative configurations as queer. While rhetorics of proximity can be invoked to engage the audience in empathetic "relations in the marginalized Other," gut-level proximities tend to operate in binaries of desires and disgust.[5] The gag reflex is an intersection of the biological, cultural, and affective messaging around consumption that can evoke literal choking or more symbolically felt sneers. One might literally gag upon eating something that violates one's sense of taste, but one can also mime a gag as an indication of how deeply felt one's distance from the disgusting object is, or should be. As such, the gag reflex marks the limit of where one feels enabled to orient in space and the distant spaces across that line that gambol with decay. This insinuated awareness of what lies beyond the threshold of disgust, a proprioceptive understanding of the self in the world, informs all rhetorical action.

The bodily processes and histories of disgust and desire are inseparable from the metaphorical structures we use to orient our affective reactions to the world. For example, in Western culture, dental hygiene is automati-

3. Frye and Bruner, *Rhetoric of Food.*
4. Ahmed, "Orientations," 547.
5. Yam, *Inconvenient Strangers,* 69.

cally perceived as such a good that the taste of mint is readily associated with cleanliness, and thus moral superiority, even though mint toothpastes and mouthwashes can cause extreme discomfort because of the application of high amounts of menthol to sensitive gum tissue. Sensations can be retconned into a positive (minty fresh!) or negative (ow, that stings) depending on the surrounding cultural expectations for the limits of bodily comfort.

Our racial geographies are in many ways overdetermined by these teachings about what we should salivate after or spit up. These naturalized reactions emerge in a variety of ways, from overt rejection to derogatory diminution, but all of these define racial and ethnic categories of food through setting levels of allowable proximity and duration of bodily attention. Ethnic food should titillate without disruption. A squeeze of sriracha rather than a whole prik jinda pepper. Anita Mannur recounts a controversy from the British reality show *Big Brother* where one of the contestants, Jade Goody, entered into an argument with Bollywood actress Shilpa Shetty; "the former launched her tirade against the actress in culinary terms, calling her 'Shilpa Poppadom,' referring to the customary appetizer served in Indian restaurants."[6] This example of crude synecdoche illustrates the unexamined warrants that undergird the relationship of race and food in the public sphere. The quick move to labeling an Indian body with a term for a trivial snack food speaks to how the bodies that produce racialized foods are often seen as synonymous with those foods by outsiders. And in that replacement, the Asian body merges with a cheap item to be greedily consumed when the white body is hungry and then blamed for indigestion afterward when the spice is too much.

In order for such synecdochic relationships between groups of people and their foodstuffs to rhetorically exclude, the relationship must be assumed to reveal a base flawed embodiment that is somehow less than normative standards for the human. A contemporary example of this orienting away from forms of consumption as a way to denigrate certain embodiments is the use of the derogatory concept "soyboy" by extremist groups connected to the "alt-right," particularly men's rights groups. The term refers to a cisgender male whose feminine appearance and behavior is a direct consequence of consuming too much soy. In a video titled "The Truth about Soy Boys" by alt-right commentator Paul Watson, he argues that the consumption of soy in "copious quantities" has resulted in not only notably lowered testosterone levels but also a vulnerability to leftist, "male feminist" ideologies. Having a "soy face"—an open-mouth smile the alt-right believes is specific to soyboys—should be mocked because it is the result of ignorant consumption choices that produce

6. Mannur, *Culinary Fictions*, 5.

a flawed physicality, according to these standards for masculinity.[7] Proponents have explicitly used this tacit belief in consumption merging with the body as a rhetorical flag that directs others away from engaging not only with soy but with those who choose to eat it. This example, while extreme, nonetheless demonstrates the rhetorical power in forwarding consumption habits, bodily comportment, and moral rubrics as coequal. Such rendering of the Other's embodiment coequal with their political position is a first step in approving violent orientations against such bodies as a means of correction to the broader sociopolitical fabric.

What I explore in this book is how these hierarchies that become attached to everyday gut feelings in service of increasing distance between bodies are key to the maintenance and reinforcement of racial and other forms of segregation. The activity of eating, when racialized, informs the knowledge and legibility of rhetorical subjects as bodies that are more or less aligned with undesirable ethics and values. As Ahmed clarifies, aspects of one's identity like race are not intrinsic in particular fleshes, "not simply determined, for example, by the 'fact' of one's skin colour," but emerge through racialization, "a process whereby bodies come to be seen, known, and lived as 'having' a racial identity."[8] Racialization, as a process of relegating attention and forgetting one has done so, leads to an ongoing *re*-relegation and *re*-preoccupation that accumulates within the body, altering our sensory judgments of the appropriateness of proximate objects and bodies. In other words, the tenuously stabilized labels of "race" and "ethnicity" are formed over time in the enaction of lived experiences, dominant discourses, media representations, and omissions. The rhetorics that define consumption through implicit and explicit references to markers of class, race, gender, and sexuality gradually become held as "truths" about racialized bodies. Care for an Other's food does not automatically erase power differentials between people. The sensational process of taking something into one's body does not equate with a more enlightened understanding of that object or the hands that make it, especially if the rhetoric that surrounds such eating processes maintains a sense of ontological difference through the digestive tract. In fact, the evocation of a strong sensory response to a food or consumable substance might be suasive *against* that food or substance because of preset norms for how bodies are supposed to interact with the eaten.

How we feel toward certain foods is a conflation of biological processes of digestion, affective inheritances from our families and broader communities, and sociorhetorical frameworks that express prominent attitudes toward

---

7. Henderson, "Inside."
8. Ahmed, "Racialized Bodies," 47.

race and racial hierarchies. The commonsense nature of these orientations, accumulated over time, lends a certain gravitas to one's physical sensations as not just individual feeling but as empirical evidence for existing racial hierarchies. Bodily attitudes that manifest in specific encounters are reverse engineered into seemingly factual generalizations about both foods and bodies. Food intertwines racial and ethnic boundaries with one's sense of one's bodily integrity, which "is significant not only because disgust is a matter of taste as well as touch—as senses that require proximity to that which is sensed—but also because food is 'taken into' the body. [. . .] The very project of survival requires we take something other into our bodies. Survival makes us vulnerable in that it requires we let what is 'not us' in."[9] The process of consumption is especially fraught with the potential for disgust because it is a reminder of the vulnerability of one's body. This reminder can cause the body to recoil from the offending object or expel it, and it is this movement away that reaffirms the object as disgusting.

Gut orientations set up presumed proximities among bodies as natural, evidenced by bodily responses to violations of these proximities. The resulting rhetorical arrangement is one in which particular bodies are not merely objectified but occupy a more liminal space as "objects *and* abjects."[10] As Edward Said maintains, the continuing appeal of "Orientalist" discourse is its unification of political, aesthetic, and economic interests, all of "which puts the Westerner in a whole series of possible relationships with the Orient without ever losing him the upper hand."[11] The resulting expectations for interrelationships and/or proximity do not necessarily demand subservience, as in the colonial context that Said was describing, but rather anticipate a certain maintained distance between bodies, objects, and their effects. Somatic responses that are "triggered by the proximity and presence of other bodies" and their foods are embedded within epistemological definitions of their presumed cultural and racial contexts, and these definitions reify the rightness of encountering those objects and abjects as marginal.[12] With Asianness in particular, the ongoing Orientalist investment in rendering a coherent and distinct Other exists at the level of bodily reaction, setting a seemingly natural baseline that limits the range and appeal of rhetorical interventions that disturb these distances and arouse such feelings.

The rhetorical weight attached to food and eating maintains subtle understandings of different types of eaters as ontologically distinct and distant. *Inscrutable Eating* contributes to the conversation surrounding the rhetori-

9. Ahmed, *Cultural Politics*, 83.
10. Yam, *Inconvenient Strangers*, 4, emphasis added.
11. Said, *Orientalism*, 7.
12. Khanna, *Visceral Logics*, 9.

cal formation of racial regimes through its investigation of how Asianness is rendered as coequal with foreignness because of dominant rhetorics of food-related decorum. The concept of gut orientations clarifies how the broader structural barriers to equity are deeply supported through the embeddedness of visceral responses to the everyday living of others as signs of natural laws rather than personal preferences. Even as discursive practices shift to reflect more inclusive intentions, there remains an ongoing uneasiness/unsettlement in the normative gut that prevents engagement even when minorities travel through the center. A critical rhetorical perspective toward race needs a gut-level analytic in order to account for how discursive and embodied attitudes toward Others are overlaid with other normative frameworks, such as those for gender and sexuality, as well as how these heuristics of inclusion and exclusion are grounded in assumptions of shared sensation. This work offers a sensory-focused rhetorical analysis that unpacks how the contradictions of the post-racial are so hard to unmoor because of their embeddedness in everyday physicalities that support a status quo racial common sense.

Focusing on the movement or fixedness implicit in matters of eating clarifies how certain proximities among groups, and their accompanying hierarchies, not only form but maintain ontological assumptions as rhetorical truths. The conversations around legacies of enslaving Black people and displacement of indigenous populations often center matters of socioeconomic lack and inequality as the prime measures of racial injustice. Scholarship on racialization within the US often focuses on the sociopolitical structures set up to incite this sort of competition among racialized communities for social prestige and material resources. Iyko Day conceptualizes how the triad of "the Native, the alien, and the settler" was developed as a model for interracial relations that supported settler colonialist logics of abstract racialized labor during the formation of the racial landscape of the US.[13] Claire Jean Kim's understanding of racial triangulation explains how Asian Americans "have been triangulated vis-à-vis Blacks and Whites through simultaneous valorization and ostracism since their first arrival in the United States."[14] As Cindy I-Fen Cheng notes, the eventual opening of US borders to Asian immigrants during the Cold War was a rhetorical maneuver designed to elevate the US as a pluralist nation, unlike Soviet countries, "that embraced people of all backgrounds."[15] Even as entrance to the US "melting pot" was promised, these new immigrants were only valued for the contrast between their foreignness and the US as a paternalistic savior. These frameworks demonstrate how racialization never occurs

13. I. Day, *Alien Capital*, 23.
14. Kim, "Racial Triangulation," 129.
15. C. Cheng, *Citizens of Asian America*, 58.

in a vacuum but rather is part of an ongoing process of affixing social values and constraints to certain identity categories in order to provide a rhetorical foil for the dominant social group. What the concept of gut orientation adds to these theories of the intersection of the economy and race is a heuristic for understanding how such attitudes endure beyond the original legislative ruling or political moment. These triangulations and oppositions are maintained not solely through socioeconomic competition but interwoven into rhetorically prominent understandings of disgust and salivation.

It is especially important to consider what attitudes about race and sensorial proximities are attached to Asian food given its widespread popularity and availability. I argue that increased access to this cuisine does not erase racial bias or is even sometimes at cross-purposes with anti-racist aims. Because food is often "situated in narratives about racial and ethnic identity as an intractable measure of cultural authenticity," its metonymic power can actually support the maintenance of racial inequity.[16] For example, Robert Ji-Song Ku explores how this dedication to finding authenticity in food, specifically Asian food, maintains the "East" and "West" as completely separate and fixed, a narrative move that erases generations of Asian American chefs and eaters as well as the flux inherent in any Asian community. As he states,

> Chinese Americans, by virtue of residing in the United States for too long, cannot qualify as bona-fide Chinese, and the food they cook up can best be described as ersatz Chinese, a poor imitation of the original, and not original in its own right. Chinese Americans, using this logic, are either poor imitations or irredeemable corruptions of the real thing; they, like their food, must therefore be considered not authentically Chinese.[17]

These debates over whether or not ethnic food is authentic essentializes Asian food as only ever one thing that must originate far from Western shores, regardless of the chef's cultural expertise, and maintains racial separation as reflecting inherent differences in bodily appetites and skills.[18] And as we will

---

16. Mannur, *Culinary Fictions*, 3.

17. Ku, *Dubious Gastronomy*, 73.

18. In an interview with Mark Wilson for *Fast Company*, chef and entertainer Andrew Zimmern infamously claimed he was "saving the souls of all the people from having to dine at these horseshit restaurants masquerading as Chinese food that are in the Midwest" by opening his own Chinese restaurant, Lucky Cricket. Zimmern stated, "I'm worried about people in Indianapolis being exposed to Chinese culture. I mean, maybe I took it on because other people haven't been able to do it. You know? I mean, was P. F. Chang's not a rip-off because Cecilia Chang's kid owned it? Because despite how he looks on the outside, he's a rich American kid on the inside. Right?" (Wilson, "Andrew Zimmern").

see in chapter 5, the question of authenticity can also be turned against the Asian eater, morphing legitimate complaints about misrepresentation into a sign of the minority who cries "reverse racism."

The gut orientations that result from Asian food's superficial popularity inscribe certain ways of encountering Asianness as not only most legible but most factual on a visceral level, a metric for race diffracted through the stomach. A different gut orientation is often required to throw into relief the sensory constructs that are assumed to make up reality. For example, the Western stereotype of Asian food as "smelly" is predicated on the belief that certain substances that are cultivated and used in certain cuisines are inherently more sensorially offensive than others. Yet sociologist Young Rae Oum offers an alternative understanding of how offense is produced amidst senses, sensitivities, and cultural expectations. Oum notes that in her experience working in childcare, just as "American schoolteachers noticed Korean kids' garlicky smell, I often found the American children smelling like fries, fish, butter, or sour milk," all foods that are common to many American diets.[19] Although we all smell (in both senses of the term), the belief that only some food substances are odorous is the result of amalgamations of cultural and culinary familiarities and the resulting gut orientations that shape our ability to recognize sensory input as either delicious or disgusting. Redefining who or what is deemed an object or abject is thus a reorientation to a different spectrum of potential sensations and actions that requires confronting the orientations that incline bodies toward or away from others. It then becomes possible to imagine alternative rhetorical possibilities.

TALKING ABOUT EATING

Discussions around food are ubiquitous, albeit differently angled depending on the discipline, arena, or medium of transmission. Public conversations on food have created some momentum for questioning assumptions about the link between consumption and identity. Shows such as *Great British Bake Off*; *Salt, Fat, Acid, Heat*; *Ugly Delicious*; *Top Chef*; *Iron Chef*; *Chopped*; and *Mind of a Chef* have contributed terminology, memes, and references to the public discourse around food. Pre–Food Network, food writers such as Michael Pollan, Anthony Bourdain, Ruth Riechl, and many others also contributed to the widespread awareness of the cultural, economic, and historical aspects of food. The rise of podcasts like *The Sporkful, Bon Appetit, Gastropod*, and *The Splendid Table* have brought more attention to issues of culture and identity

---

19. Oum, "Authenticity and Representation," 110.

into public discourse. Celebrity chefs such as David Chang, Anthony Bourdain, Edourado Jordan, and Samrin Nosrat have spoken about where race, gender, and labor intersect in their kitchens and in the restaurant industry more broadly. Such discussions are necessarily incomplete and are just starting to address how the intertwining of food and economics means that usually, certain bodies are allowed to consume and enjoy, and certain bodies are expected to "be continually exoticized until they reach the point of incommensurability."[20] These often unvoiced expectations nonetheless feed socioeconomic inequities in terms of who is seen as having earned both authority and a higher paycheck.[21]

Historically, food's ongoing role as a key signifier and socioeconomic driver of national development and inclusion has often resulted in contestation and violence. Scholars such as Joshua Specht and Melanie DuPuis trace how the material and symbolic conflict enacted in supply chains and nutrition shaped the contours of modern beliefs about food and American values during Westward expansion and beyond.[22] These historical events have directly influenced contemporary rhetorical formations of health and eating, as many now taken-for-granted ideas about the American diet are beholden to "moral biopolitics of [various] American reform movements" from the nineteenth and twentieth centuries.[23] Similarly, Charlotte Biltekoff details how advice about diet and "eating right" fosters a culture of hyperfocus on individual decisions and self-control, ignoring the range of environmental and socioeconomic constraints that make certain embodiments unachievable for many.[24] The rhetorical positioning of food and eaters always creates material impact through creating layers of inclusion and exclusion that limit access to both food itself and any available cultural capital.

Because of its cultural power, discussing food is crucial for understanding the tension between marginalization and fetishization. Scholars in cultural studies and Asian American studies explore how representations of minority food are key factors in the spatial and rhetorical arrangements of entire communities, from the siloing of certain forms of labor along racial lines, cordoning off certain populations as tainted consumers in discourse around public health, or defining of deviant bodies in opposition to moral citizenship.[25] In his discussion of the colonization of the Philippines, René Alexander Orquiza

20. Kelly, *Food Television*, 40.
21. Rao, "Bon Appétit Video."
22. See Specht, *Red Meat Republic* and DuPuis, *Dangerous Digestion*.
23. DuPuis, *Dangerous Digestion*, 4.
24. Biltekoff, *Eating Right in America*.
25. See Xu, *Eating Identities*; Ku, Manalansan, and Mannur, *Eating Asian America*; Ray, *Ethnic Restaurateur*; Shah, *Contagious Divides*; and Tompkins, *Racial Indigestion*.

Jr. details how American colonizers crafted narratives of American cuisine as a resource of moral and sociological uplift for the native population, in contrast to the supposed squalor of local dishes, feeding a market for imported American foodstuffs at the expense of local traditions.[26] Social justice and the alimentary are always entwined.

Rhetorical scholarship on food takes up the contradictions of geography, identity, and culture through analyzing which narratives of food and eating seem more persuasive than others and how they circulate. Or, the stories we tell about other peoples' food directly influence the stories we tell about other people. Casey Ryan Kelly engages how our understanding of the global, and therefore race and ethnicity, is mediated through portrayals of global cuisine. Kelly focuses on how dominant media portrayals misrepresent "Other" cultures' foodways according to tacit white supremacist assumptions about hygiene and flavor.[27] Similarly, the goal in the collection *Food, Feminisms, and Rhetorics* is to spotlight long-standing gender and sexual bias in food practices by taking the reader through a reconsideration of overlooked food texts and artifacts, such as handwritten recipe notecards, and reevaluating what rhetoric considers to be valid objects and methods of analysis.[28] Donovan Conley and Justin Eckstein challenge the field to deeply consider how dominant rhetorics mask what goes into food processing and infrastructure.[29] In her study of recipe headnotes, Tippen considers how the seeding of small, seemingly inconsequential details about these authors' lives and histories shapes views of Southern life and identity for non-Southerners.[30] These sorts of explorations and their focus on national or regional identity sketch how what is prioritized and what is omitted in the political imaginary of eaters creates lasting shifts that trickle upward to understandings of local and national geographies. Such works recuperate lost or overlooked narratives and practices, expose rhetorical misrepresentations of food and culture, and search for exemplar texts that offer more positive ways of engaging with difference.

What I add to this ongoing conversation around the performance of race, citizenship, and food is an understanding of rhetoric as, in addition to visuals, screens, and texts, the enduring affects that accrue in and around the bodies that engage with such artifacts. I argue we must consider how these dominant presences in mainstream discourses and visuals accumulate within the bodies of those watching and eating, inclining audiences' bodies toward or away

---

26. Orquiza, *Taste of Control.*
27. Kelly, *Food Television.*
28. Goldthwaite, *Food, Feminisms, Rhetorics.*
29. Conley and Eckstein, *Cookery.*
30. Tippen, *Inventing Authenticity.*

from certain flavors and practices.[31] So, if rhetoric is about moving others from a previously held position toward a new one, attending to gut orientations explains some of the bodily baggage that gets in the way of seeing a new position as not only within reach but also adding value. You cannot engage what you do not recognize. With this in mind, I analyze racialized rhetorics of food with an eye for how ongoing messages around food accumulate into normative ways of being and relating. Food, as a sensual medium, exerts rhetorical force beyond the singular representation in a meal or a television program. Racialized and racist discourses are persuasive because of unexamined concatenations of ways of moving and feeling in relation to Others that are reinforced by arguments about the right and wrong ways to eat.

To clarify how gut orientations muddy the rhetorical waters around race, I unpack how the tacit affective principles embedded in prominent discourses and images around food coalesce over time into assumptions about preset, unchanging racialized ontologies. The misrepresentations, or reductive representations, of food and food cultures continue to occur because there are certain "right" ways of feeling around food that circulate in everyday rhetorical texts and expected bodily performances. The beliefs about which racial groups are more or less clean, and therefore more or less moral, are felt in affective reactions to what does or not belong on one's plate, or who does or does not belong at which table. My case studies focus on how societal expectations for gut, sensorial reactions are used to shore up distances between groups of people—*we* all feel the same feelings of disgust, which demonstrates that *they* are disgusting—and block critical consideration of the assumptions that support ongoing misunderstandings rather than an honest sharing of epistemological difference.

Investigating the banal, yet potent, area of eating and consumption clarifies many of the rhetorical mechanisms that support the continued identification of Asian Americans as a perpetual outsider, a present absence in the racial imaginary. Scholars such as Jo Hsu, Lu Ming Mao, Terese Guinsatao Monberg, LeiLani Nishime, Kent Ono, Vincent Pham, Jennifer Sano-Franchini, Shui-Yin Sharon Yam, and Morris Young (among many others) have analyzed various forms of oppressive and liberatory rhetoric that constrain or enable attention to rhetorical concerns about Asians and Asian Americans. These scholarly

---

31. My understanding of how exactly to define rhetoric is varied, reflecting some of the field's debates over what keywords or emphases should be most central, but the main hub of my thinking about rhetoric aligns with definitions centered on movement and energy, how rhetorical "things" create pushes and pulls in the world that bear seeds of potential transformation and paths of potential action, either with or against others. I am indebted to Debra Hawhee's emphasis on "the training and production of a rhetorical subject" as a way into thinking through the body as a site impacted by and for enaction of rhetorical praxis (*Bodily Arts*, 16).

efforts address the misrepresentation of Asian and Asian American rhetors in education and public discourse, demonstrating both where Asianness has always been present but undiscussed and where more efforts are needed to bring these voices into the conversation. Particularly, the aim for much of this work is to "use the symbolic resources of language in social, cultural, and political arenas to disrupt and transform the dominant European American discourse and its representations of Asians and Asian Americans."[32] The rhetorical project of preventing bodies from moving in and through spaces is often based on narratives that encourage a sort of affective segregation, cued not just by barbed wire or redlining but by gut-level recoils from contact with objects and bodies that are, in Mary Douglas's terms, "matter out of place."[33] In order to achieve the productive disruptions and transformations that Mao and Young call for, we need to more fully apprehend how prominent rhetorics that exclude or elide Asianness are rooted in gut orientations that encourage distance from it.

To demonstrate this link between gut-level feelings and racial hierarchies, I turn to arguments about consumption made in the US public sphere, both historical and contemporary, and analyze how they rhetorically position Asian bodies in relation to white norms via judgments about attraction and repulsion to foodstuffs. These arguments emerge within what Michael McGee labeled the "fragments" of public discourse and hold authority based on their continued circulation and recirculation, rather than solely on the ethos of an original rhetor or rhetorical event.[34] Once in circulation, the visceral power of these metaphoric discussions couples an activation of latent prejudices with sensory "evidence" for the rightness of those judgments. Appetite is the sum of the physiological realities of metabolism and calorie consumption, but it is also "a rhetorical effect, a product of the values inherent in the ways food is discussed" in the overlap of private tasting and public speaking.[35] An appetite for, or the converse of disgust for, enacts racial hierarchies through naturalized affective responses and rhetorical rationales for said responses.

QUEER MOUTHS AND THEIR FEELINGS

In untangling these explicit signals of disgust and tacit assumptions about proper food hygiene, it is immediately evident how "relations of power are

32. Mao and Young, *Representations*, 2.
33. Douglas, *Purity and Danger*, 36.
34. McGee, "Text, Context."
35. Eckstein and Young, "wastED Rhetoric," 286.

interwoven with other kinds of relations" that "delineate general conditions of domination" throughout the public sphere in conversations about something as seemingly banal as food.[36] These relations of power mark the racialized body both as one that consumes disgusting objects and one that *desires* disgusting objects. To encounter such a body is therefore to risk contact with the disgusting substance itself as well as the potentially corrupting influence of the slavering, nondiscerning eater. Specifically, the discourse centered on the consumption practices offers insight into how the Asian body is rhetorically constructed as that which is always out of step from other racial ontologies through metrics of everyday feeling and desire.

Traditionally, rhetoric is related to questions of identity and community, how we call for or deny ways of "acting-together" through discourse, visuals, embodiments, and technologies. How do you persuade someone to not only be on your side in one battle but also continue to fight for your cause with vigor?[37] There are clearly resonances between judgments about what one chooses to consume and finding your tribe of substantively similar people; "substance, in the old philosophies, was an *act*; and a way of life is an *acting-together*; and in acting together, men have common sensations, concepts, images, ideas, attitudes that make them *consubstantial.*"[38] The focus on substance as it operates in relation to food and eating is key; everyone should have a substantively similar enough reaction to a food, both in terms of the initial desire or disgust and what it does within one's body. Eating together therefore always bears the potential to threaten heteronormative bodies and national boundaries with deviance that might mar one's ability to remain in the dominant identity category.[39]

36. Foucault, *Power/Knowledge*, 132.

37. See Lyon, *Deliberative Acts* and Ratcliffe, *Rhetorical Listening* for critiques of Burke's theory. While I recognize the theoretical richness of these critiques, I am focused here on the processes that make racial identifications more or less appealing according to dominant rubrics, rather than on the coherence of Burke's body of work. To that end, a Burkean understanding of identity helps illustrate how societal hierarchies are made to *feel* natural and coherent in everyday performance. Performances of identification are necessarily incomplete in order to achieve consistency across a group of individuals, but that internal lack of validity is what makes policing the boundaries of the identity category all the more exigent.

38. Burke, *Rhetoric of Motives*, 21.

39. Finding connections with other cultures via food can have positive effects; Vivian Nun Halloran writes in *The Immigrant Kitchen* about how autobiographical narratives of food and eating can help demystify myths and stereotypes of immigrant populations. Yet these positive reading experiences can mask how consumption is "a complex, at times, contradictory cultural economy that links identity politics to the production of labor and the exchange of commodities for social values that the body performs" (see Fung, "Teaching Food and Foodways," ii).

Just as racism "is the 'feeling' that articulates and keeps the flawed logic of race in its place," prejudices against nonnormative performances of gender and sexuality emerge from gut orientations that hold certain forms of sensing and sensation as too much and therefore crossing the line into queer deviance.[40] Karma Chávez puts it bluntly: The "preservation of whiteness literally depends on heterosexuality and appropriate gender norms, creating an interwoven relationship between the 'nation-as-white' and the 'nation-as-heterosexual' that leads to policing of all kinds of borders," whether at national borders or the seeming limits of the individual body.[41] These mutually supportive constructions of whiteness, heteronormativity, and heterosexuality produce queerness not solely in relation to sexual behavior but as a looming threat to normative embodiment more generally. Therefore, any analysis of how race and racism circulate and recur must also be aware of how multiple identities are made to overlap and support particular versions of each other in service of norms. Randall Halle defines queerness not through a taxonomy of particular bodily acts but through attending to "the coercive norms that place [queer people's] desire into a position of conflict with the present order."[42] Defining queerness as desires out of step with the dominant social order is useful for thinking through where assumed inherencies are at the root of rhetoric used to label certain bodies as conflicting with normative expectations. These pathologized "symptoms" can be reverse engineered into whole bodies, which means they can be wielded alongside a range of taxonomies, offering examples of deviance that can be attached to whichever categories—gender, race, or sexuality—are under suspicion. Just as performances of gender and sexuality are taken up as autonomous choices and inherent desires, the taking of something into one's body can quickly transform from a matter of survival to a revelation of unimaginable inner cravings.

In the rhetorics wielded around consumption, fear around what can enter or exit the body is tied to a fear of queer sexual behavior but also suspicions of a broader deviance of flesh. As in the homophobic myth that "homosexual degeneracy inherently embodies desire for the vulnerable young, compulsion sated by their allurement and molestation," consumption of things with repellent tastes and textures is proffered as evidence of bodies that always use themselves wrongly, rupturing the appropriate boundaries between the inside and outside in ways that leak and contaminate those in close proximity.[43] Suspicion of queerness is suspicion of "bodies that don't cohere according

---

40. Holland, *Erotic Life*, 6.
41. Chávez, *Queer Migration Politics*, 11.
42. Halle, *Queer Social Philosophy*, 117.
43. Morris, "Sunder the Children," 405.

to cis-centric, sexually dimorphic, ableist conceptions of somatic normalcy."[44] The boundaries drawn around consumption in service of "somatic normalcy" assume queerness as a coherent, unified ontology of brokenness that directly opposes straight norms. An accusation of queerness is never just about sexual practices, deviant consumption, or suspect ancestry but a marking of one behavior that is supposedly hiding a dozen related others.

Repeatedly, rhetorics surrounding Asians and their fit within the West draw on deviance of eating as evidence of deeper freakishness of embodiment, and the tacit expectation is that audiences will feel the appropriate level of repulsion from all such bodies in response. As demonstrated in the following case studies, the focus on trouble with racialized eaters is indebted to implicit assumptions of queer embodiment as catching. If the dominant envisioning of Asianness in the public sphere is of an innately deficient and/or offensive embodiment, creating rhetorics related to Asian life bears the burden of first issuing correctives to these ongoing unsound archetypes. While I center race in these analyses, it is impossible to ignore how the formation of Asianness is intertwined with normalizing pressures on the performance of gender and sexuality.

FORGETTING GUT ORIENTATIONS

Michael Lacy and Kent Ono remind us that contemporary racism's subtlety is its rhetorical strength. Therefore, in addition to denouncing overt forms of discrimination, a critical rhetorical perspective requires looking for the "inferential forms of race and racism" in "mundane, everyday, and routine cultural practices."[45] Because I understand narratives of racial and sexual hierarchy as reasserting dominance in terms of intellect *and* physicality, via ideology *and* affect,[46] I argue one must understand not only discourses of inequality but

44. Malatino, *Queer Embodiment*, 2.

45. Lacy and Ono, *Critical Rhetorics*, 3.

46. There are ongoing debates as to the limits or focus of affect theory. These competing and overlapping foci fall into roughly eight strands that are found in a variety of disciplinary contexts; see Gregg and Seigworth, *Affect Theory Reader*. Many strands center the freeing, autonomous power of circulating affect as a way out of the traps of post-structuralism. Brian Massumi asserts that the "autonomy of affect is [. . .] its openness" that "escapes confinement in the particular body" (*Parables*, 35). Erin Manning's definition of affect as "the with-ness of the movement of the world" (*Politics of Touch*, xxi) is brilliantly evocative in its rooting of affect in the interchange among bodies and environments. These sorts of conceptions of affect tend to follow Spinoza and his prioritization of the encounter, and it makes sense why much of rhetoric's uptake of affect has transposed the interest in the relations and forces within the encounter as a more embodied version of the rhetorical situation.

also the associated embodiments and inhabitations that support the existence of such discourses. We can then see how repetition of such narratives creates a sense of physical rightness that comes from occupying the right/white space. This seemingly commonsense orientation toward bodies and objects is embedded through performative repetition that masks itself; "the labor of repetition disappears through labor: if we work hard at something, then it seems effortless."[47] Certain acculturations not only prioritize ideological positions over others but also render those positions affectively and physically more comfortable and therefore harder to recognize as arbitrary.[48] These orientations inform which epistemologies dominate in the field and elsewhere. As multiple scholars have noted, the implicitly white orientation of scholarship replicates societal hierarchies that determine "who moves with the least friction and the most favor in the field of rhetoric."[49] Movement here is both metaphorical and literal; representation on the page is not a mere mimicry of embodiment but inclines the reading body toward different ways of encountering in text and the flesh.

In other words, to be raced or gendered or sexualized is to be part of an ongoing pedagogical project, and one of the main teachers is the gut reactions formed in the repeated re-placing of one's body in relation to norms and the successive bodily experiences of flight or rest. These perceptions are both informed and affirmed by "past experience, by biopolitics, and micropolitical techniques that educate affects, habits, and disposition," all of which prepare the body for particular forms of engagement as not just advantageous but also morally elevated and emotionally comfortable.[50] Debra Hawhee points out how rhetorical bodily intelligence is developed through imitation of successful physical models. In other words, "one knows healthy walking when one sees it, precisely because one has seen a healthy person walking many times before."[51] The broader set of bodily encounters and recognitions that situate our understanding of appropriate physical performances are rooted in an aware enough mimesis that allows for a pivot to rhetorical amplification and extension.

---

47. Ahmed, *Cultural Politics*, 246.

48. In the many conversations that have accompanied #BlackLivesMatter protests, many Black parents have described the talks they have with their children about interacting with police or other authority figures. They explicitly train their children in physical and affective behavior in response to dominant orientations toward Blackness that express themselves in both hate speech and visceral fear. White parents have responded with disbelief that such a horrendous task could be part of parenting in the contemporary US, in part because such an orientation toward the world feels so strange.

49. Chávez, "The Body," 245.

50. Swanton, "Sorting Bodies," 2347.

51. Hawhee, *Bodily Arts*, 153.

Such an ontoepistemological understanding of bodily habituation helps us see how the cornerstones of rhetorical thought (the dexterity of *mētis*, the keen awareness of topoi, the solidity of identification, the rightness of certain metaphors, the retrospective obviousness of kairos) are made viable through processes of bodily conditioning that render certain orientations to the world as more sensical and appealing than others. The choreography that makes race *feel* real, the "*process of materialization that stabilizes over time to produce the effect of boundary, fixity, and surface we call matter,*" is an ongoing manifestation of intercorporeal and intracorporeal relationships that are only questioned when the connective tissue between racial, gendered, and/or sexual categories contracts or expands enough to disturb the status quo.[52] A body's rhetorical power is thus mediated through both physical and ideological proprioceptive ranges that orient us toward certain configurations of actors, spacings, and alignments as both physically and morally proper. As a simple example, we might think about the common kindergarten exercise of "criss-cross applesauce," the folding of legs and crossing of arms that follow the verbal cue, as both a way of containing the physical energy of four-year-olds and also a habituation where physical stillness is equal to moral self-control. The wrestling of one's body into a criss-crossed contortion is both an obedience to social norms and a performance of Aristotle's "healthy man walking" that engages the self and others in ongoing reaffirmation of these norms.

Habituated affect accustoms bodies to certain proximities that are bound up with implicit understandings of the consumptive power, and associated threat, of bodies. When this set of feelings, objects, and feelers has been repeated enough to coalesce into a recognizable orientation, rather than merely a personal preference attached to a singular body, it holds trope-ic force because the process of habituation has been forgotten. The "social act of seeing race deploys our bodily senses that have been collectively and historically trained and cultivated to see, hear, and *confirm* race as a source of differences that matter."[53] In other words, narratives of race and racism are bound up with the physiological processes of inhabiting a body shot through with history, culture, and material influence. Different forms of inhabiting one's own body entrain only certain affects and related physicalities as normative, limiting one's scope for rhetorical understanding of the presumed Other and foreclosing access to other forms of embodiment.

Attention to what gut orientations help us recognize clarifies how such constellations of race come to be dominant through the patterned enactment of visceral feelings, and it also gives us more specific language of proxim-

---

52. Butler, *Bodies That Matter*, 69.
53. Sekimoto, "Race and the Senses," 91.

ity and distance, attraction and repulsion, that helps decipher how the daily enactment of these configurations inheres in bodies in ways both particular and contradictory. As Ahmed emphasizes, some "objects do not even become objects of perception since the body does not move toward them: they are 'beyond the horizon' of the body, out of reach."[54] Especially when thinking about race and interpersonal interaction, it is less often the case that a group of bodies is completely missing from public consciousness but rather that the incentives for moving close enough to that which is "out of reach" are absent.

In the case of bodies deemed unassailably queer in race, behavior, and flesh, gut orientations provide connective mesh that encapsulates these separate negative beliefs into a unified-enough set of repulsed feelings against a fictional Other that feels not only real but dangerous. Just as Orientalist discourses "created the Orient (and Orientals) as objects of knowledge and representation, whether in sympathy or with hostility," the formation of Asian eaters as always queerly raced and gendered makes it possible to identify and delegitimize certain bodies as simultaneously repulsive and allowable in proper society due to non or extra-human traits.[55] These ongoing, unchallenged narratives of deviant consumption enable detrimental rhetorical identifications to bloom in the undergrowth, not always manifesting in overt racial violence but maintaining a sense of general unease. Enacting rhetoric from within or adjacent to Asianness thus requires negotiating not only the exigencies of a particular spatiotemporal moment but also the preexisting judgments that might incline an audience a bit further away to begin with.

THE CONTRADICTION OF POST-RACIAL ASIANNESS

In thinking through how Asianness is formed through rhetorics of consumption, it is especially important to consider how previous eras' explicit Othering of Asianness dovetails with proclamations of the "post-racial" era. For many Americans, the election of Barack Obama as the US president in 2008 seemed to herald a new era where race was no longer a barrier to entry, even to the most powerful position in the nation, and therefore is "something incidental that frankly no longer matters and is, in general, simply unspeakable."[56] The discourse in the public sphere shifted to asking, and then claiming, that we were now in an era where race was no longer a structural hurdle. Finally, we could quit with the "identity politics" and focus on merit. The post-racial

54. Ahmed, *Queer Phenomenology*, 55.
55. Chong, "Orientalism," 183.
56. De Genova, "'War on Terror,'" 259.

offers affective comfort for what are "felt as threats to the imaginary and symbolic status of masculine whiteness" from nonnormative gender and racial identities.[57] Despite the claims of this post-racial context, Asian Americans are still saddled with the "model minority" myth, the narrative that Asians, whether for biological or cultural reasons, are a group "whose cultural values of diligence, family solidarity, respect for education, and self-sufficiency have propelled it to notable success."[58] As other minorities are sold on the idea that "yellow is a shade of white and that blacks and browns (Latinos) could improve their economic status if only they adopted some 'yellow' characteristics," Asians are encouraged to lighten their skin and behavior even further via brightening creams and assimilative silences.[59] The poet Cathy Park Hong describes the problems these understandings of Asian American life causes.

> It's a unique condition that's distinctly Asian, in that some of us are economically doing better than any other minority group but we barely exist anywhere in the public eye. [. . .] Asians are the invisible serfs of the garment and service industries, exposed to third-world work conditions and subminimum wages, but it's assumed that the only group beleaguered by the shrinking welfare state is working-class whites. But when we complain, Americans suddenly know everything about us. *Why are you pissed? You're next in line to be white!* As if we're iPads queued up in an assembly line.[60]

The comparison of Asian bodies to iPads is snarky but apt in that the Asian body is still always thought of in relation to that which is easily consumed. In order to access the mainstream, the Asianness of the product must be diminished enough, assimilated enough, to be rendered palatable to a white audience and a white market. Yet as Hong points out, the rhetoric that paints assimilation as a matter of individual behavior necessarily ignores global systems of exploitation and inequality that operate according to tacit intersectional hierarchies.[61] The myth's emphasis on Asians as hardworking capitalists "erases a long history of institutionalized exclusion by characterizing Asian American success precisely as the result—rather than something that occurred

---

57. Watts, "Postracial Fantasies," 318.

58. Kim, "Racial Triangulation," 118.

59. Hattori and Ching, "Reexamining," 54. See also Bow, *Partly Colored* and Washington, *Blasian Invasion.*

60. Hong, *Minor Feelings,* 19.

61. See Lowe, *Immigrant Acts* for a discussion of how Asian immigrant women in low-paid factory jobs and other menial work are often rendered invisible in dominant narratives of Asian American identity.

despite the lack—of equal opportunity."[62] It also papers over the very different histories of varying Asian ethnic groups and their ability to assimilate into the US thus far; as recently as 2018, Asian Americans were the racial group with the highest level of income disparity among different ethnic groups.[63]

Despite its encapsulation of "racist love," the model minority myth remains a rhetorically powerful scaffold of white supremacist assumptions, welding together the belief that Asians are unique among minorities in terms of intellect and culture, thus proving the rightness of the meritocracy, with the assumption that Asians' natural embodying of white-adjacent qualities proves a lack of racism in the US public sphere.[64] The backhanded compliment of this "next in line" status frames Asians as both passive and potentially exceptional, a status that continually reifies the Asian's status as an outsider in the US. To be rhetorically useful and socially acceptable, the Asian American must stay *Asian* to stay set apart from both other minority groups and the white mainstream.

While much of the contemporary discourse on Asians and Asian Americans tends to align with the model minority trope of achievement and passivity, the enactment of this trope via beliefs in food and consumption also resurrects prior tropes of the "perpetual foreigner" or "yellow peril" as needed. These multiple categorizations of Asianness are necessarily contradictory, but the belief in a flawed embodiment as evidenced by deviant eating practices enables a sliding among these tropes as is most rhetorically advantageous. In the following chapters, we will see how the rhetorical process of maintaining affinity for existing racial boundaries within the gut draws on these various images with different intensities as is needed for the recentering of whiteness. Throughout all of these operations, what remains consistent is a denigration of the elements associated with Asian embodiment related to taste, sensation, and emotional expression.

Gut orientations toward race often emerge as discourses around inherent levels of morality and taste on the part of eaters, as in how fried chicken and Spam became cornerstones of diets in the South and Hawai'i due to legacies of slavery and colonialism yet are now held up as evidence of these populations' unhealthy nature and indiscriminate palates.[65] In the case of Asian Americans, the thought is often that "perhaps Asians are 'naturally' great cooks, just as they are popularly perceived as 'innately' good at math."[66] This compliment,

62. Eng and Han, *Racial Melancholia*, 41.
63. Kochhar and Cilluffo, "Income Inequality."
64. Bow, *Racist Love*, 5.
65. Twitty, *The Cooking Gene*.
66. Ku, Manalansan, and Mannur, *Eating Asian America*, 1.

when reiterated as one of the main identifiers of Asian culture, masks the practice and skill of cooking and depicts Asian food as always tasty but also in the position of Plato's proverbial "knack," never as fine cuisine. The more pressing issue with these sorts of food-related racial essentialisms is how they easily merge with racist stereotypes. Just as Asians are "naturally" great chefs, "the irksome question Asian Americans often confront: 'Do you eat dogs?'" signals how this racial essentialism slides into a crude form of Othering based on presumed gustatory desires.[67]

My hope is that this investigation of bodily habits related to consumption and the associated limits on the expression of Asian identity will enable us to rethink what we mean by racial justice, to demand more of the American imagined community than a mere lack of harm to bodies that dare to perform a less popular ethnic identity. Rather, unfixing the entrainment of racism in our bodily orientations requires work on the rhetorical postures that angle away from where identity and oppression intersect in the everyday. As seen in the complexities of contemporary social justice movements, the difficult unpacking of overlapping forms of domination is necessary for a deeper form of work on inequity and injustice. For example, many in the #BlackLivesMatter movement are working to highlight how structural violence impacts a range of Black bodies and identities in addition to the Black men whose deaths are most circulated. Activists of color are building on the awareness of sexual assault that resulted from #MeToo to call attention to how anti-female violence is also often anti-trans and anti-BIPOC. #StopAsianHate has just begun to highlight how the recent violence against Asian Americans is part of a broader pattern of sociopolitical omission and denigration. Racial violence is always supported by prejudices against other identity categories, which means that overt forms of oppression are enmeshed in more implicit judgments about appropriate forms of embodiment. The case studies in this book demonstrate how the judgments surrounding Asian food and Asian eaters operate under the guise of appropriate and/or hygienic eating while also smuggling in judgments about gender, sexuality, and class that support current social hierarchies. This book seeks to uncover these social heuristics that render everyday microaggressive attitudes against Asian and consumption practices as an acceptable part of racial hygiene even as conversations about racial justice flourish.

---

67. Ku, Manalansan, and Mannur, *Eating Asian America*, 2.

CHAPTER 2

Rat Eaters

Defining American Masculinity in Opposition to Asian Deviance

If it was believed that Chinese relished eating rats, it was not difficult
to imagine them capable of consuming anything and everything.
—John Kuo Wei Tchen, *New York before Chinatown*

A common American folk song from the late 1800s paints a sneering picture
of a "Chinaman," a character worth mocking both because of his economic
misfortune and his bizarre eating habits.

> Chinkie, Chinkie, Chinaman
> Sitting on the fence,
> Trying to make a dollar
> Out of fifteen cents.
> Chink, Chink, Chinaman
> Eats dead rats
> Eats them up
> Like gingersnaps.

There are many versions of this folk rhyme circulating in the public sphere.
Folklorists have found several instances of similar ditties "from the 1880s
through the 1960s that are similar to 'Chink Chink Chinaman' and were most
likely used to tease and harass Chinese immigrant men."[1] As late as 1945, John
Steinbeck's version in *Cannery Row* was

---

1. Moon, *Yellowface*, 136.

Ching Chong, Chinaman,
Sitting on a rail.
Along came a white man,
And chopped off his tail.

Most versions of this song involve the "Chinaman" coming to some form of
bodily harm. In this version, the fate of the Chinaman is a kind of castration, the removal of his long hair braid, otherwise known as a queue, often
derogatorily labeled a "tail." While the hairstyle originated as a sign of submis-
sion to the then ruling Manchu government, it transformed into both a self-
claimed sign of Chinese male identity for these new immigrants and a visual
alert for white anxieties about appropriate performances of gender, sexuality,
and national allegiance. The investment in understanding the Chinese body
as bearing rat-like characteristics is part of a broader gut orientation toward
Asian masculinity as that which is a deviant contradiction, simultaneously
successful at the masculine project of financial competition while failing at
other markers of heteronormative strength and patriarchal headship. In order
to rhetorically neutralize the Asian male, the "Chinaman," as both eater of rats
and bearer of rat-like qualities, is rendered just human enough to be looked
down upon for his wrongful consumption and embodiment. So, in the rhetorical hierarchy of subjects, "objects and abjects," the Asian male is cast as a
rat-like abject, a deformed form of masculinity that proves the superiority of
white manhood through its unassimilable nature.[2]

In order to render this abjection persuasive, the particular flavor of this
anti-Chinese rhetoric revolves around the idea of a body that is continually
recontaminated by its repeated consumption of food not fit for humans, to
the point of one's body transforming into something akin to that object. This
repulsive habit is presented as inseparable from other slovenly mental and
physical qualities, such as sitting on a rail (sloth) and trying to make a dollar
out of fifteen cents (greed, stupidity). The description of how Chinese people
supposedly eat these soiled foods offers the strongest evidence for shunning
this method of consumption and the bodies that use it. Eating rats "like gin-
gersnaps," like a sugary treat, evokes a sense of embodiment that is rapid,
unthinking, and marked by a lack of self-control. Gobbling dead rats like
cookies means that these individuals have not only fundamentally different
taste buds but a very different set of bodily proclivities that find pleasure in
strange circumstances. The linkage between Chinese and vermin was rhetorically deployed to demonstrate how the US's "body politic" itself is threatened
by the influx of outsiders that are indigestible, "those who did not agree with

2. Yam, *Inconvenient Strangers*, 4.

the national stomach."[3] The half-eaten rat is only the most visible point of difference.

Contact between Chinese and Americans within the 1800s was fraught with contradictions of desire, prestige, and economic competition. For white Americans, the economic power that came from trading with China was accompanied by the cultural power of owning and displaying expensive goods such as tea, silk, and crockery, all modified for Western taste and customs.[4] Every fashionable household needed to have the familiar blue and white porcelain of the Yuan dynasty prominently displayed to show their cosmopolitan mindset (and depth of pocket). Anne Anlin Cheng points out that this obsession with ornate Chinoiserie bled into, and is now often synonymous with, the presumed gleaming allure of the Asian feminine, "whose condition of objectification is often the very hope for any claims she might have to value or personhood.[5] In contrast, the Asian masculine was originally defined through its relationship to hard labor. Thousands of Chinese men immigrated to seek their luck in the California Gold Rush, and the cornerstone of the US's explosive economic growth, the Transcontinental Railroad, would not have been possible except for the labor of these men.

As these Chinese men were immigrating, the overall rapid changes to the racial landscape of the US amplified the now upended expectations for appropriate interracial proximities in the workforce. The influx of formerly enslaved Black workers and new immigrants from Europe and Asia threatened the racial dominance of white men in the workforce; by 1880, 80 percent of the New York City population was immigrants, making up to two-thirds of the labor force in mining and manufacturing by 1910.[6] The arrival of the new settlers from Asia in particular "undermined the definition of Oriental difference, which relied on distance."[7] The resulting racist misrepresentations and caricatures that tended to focus on the "swarming" and "flooding" of these invaders were rhetorical responses aimed at resetting the proper proximal relationships between white and Asian bodies by drawing a line in the sand between the individuals who would contribute to the new nation and those who would strangle its nascent growth.[8] First, Asian women were shut out of the country via the Page Act of 1875, which was directly aimed at barring

---

3. Councilor, "Feeding the Body," 142.
4. Davis, *Chinese Lady,* 123.
5. A. Cheng, *Ornamentalism,* xii.
6. Mink, *Old Labor,* 48–49.
7. R. Lee, *Orientals,* 28.
8. In *Yellow Peril,* John Kuo Wei Tchen and Dylan Yeats point out how in several different eras of anti-Asian sentiment, the visual representations of the threat often rely on octopus-like imagery, the many tentacles of economic might and racial impurity seeking to strangle white workers' futures.

Chinese women, all labeled as prostitutes, from entering the US. Eventually, the supposed exigency of foreign competition for both jobs and control over the national moral arc grew pressing enough that the Chinese Exclusion Act was passed in 1882, setting a legal precedent that defined "*race in relation to other immigrant groups*" and US national sovereignty in explicit opposition to foreign immigration.[9] The aspirational growth of the US did not include Asian families.

At the same time, the definition of white masculinity as equated with one's ability to labor and provide for a heteronormative familial unit was increasingly untenable as more and more markedly foreign immigrants increased competition and appeared to drive down wages. The blame for this perceived competition rests with the managerial class, who incentivized Chinese immigration even while paying these workers a fraction of what they paid white workers. For these bosses, such as railroad barons Charles Crocker and Leland Stanford, Chinese workers were not "slaves" or "workers" but rather "pets," a term that conjured up an "image of loyalty and controllability."[10] In response to this docile, tamed version of animality, anti-Chinese and pro-laborer groups used visceral imagery of rats and soiled consumption in order to normalize distance between white and Asian workers by creating metonymic connections between Asian bodies and rats, portraying Chinese individuals as part of a broader category of Asian eaters, quick to devour that which violated Western norms for unclean foods.[11] The focus on these forms of consumption was also connected to the dominant portrayal of Chinese men as "nonreproductive, perverse, and feminized," abject in both sexual desires and gut hungers.[12] Especially given that the Page Act had created immense gender disparity in the groups of Asian immigrants, with many male migrants sending money to families back home, a new fear arose around potential miscegenation between Asian men and white women. The fears of this contaminating proximity to Asianness/vulnerability of whiteness were rhetorically packaged in a metonymic linkage between the Chinese and rat eater, unable to over-

9. E. Lee, "Chinese Exclusion Example," 56, emphasis added.

10. Cheung, "Anxious and Ambivalent," 294.

11. An 1883 article in the *New York Times*, titled "Mott Street Chinamen Angry: They Deny That They Eat Rats," covers a dispute between Chung Kee, also known as Mr. Wong, and a Dr. Charles Kammerer. Dr. Kammerer reportedly saw a Chinese neighbor of a friend "handling some things that looked like very small cats or very large rats" and accused Mr. Wong of butchering cats and rats and then throwing their corpses into a neighbor's yard. Despite the lack of evidence for rat/cat consumption, the article discusses in great detail the many ways in which Chinese are presumed to be associated with rats, either in terms of cooking or untoward handling of the corpses.

12. I. Day, *Alien Capital*, 86.

come inherent desires for unnatural forms of consumption, fixing Asian bodies as predetermined toward moral turpitude.

Through examining historical artifacts that center on the Chinese-rat metonymy, we see how the gut is transformed into a key battleground for racial purity through calling on fears of bodily permeability and racial contamination. In this chapter, I briefly contextualize how the rapid expansion of industry shifted the available forms of labor, upending existing definitions of ideal masculinity. I rhetorically analyze folk songs and other popular media artifacts of the time in order to excavate how fears about the status of the white male laborer gradually became linked causally to the threat of the rat-like Chinese foreigner. This rendering of Chinese men as consuming and/or being rats allows a rhetorical flexibility, at times enabling a blaming of the Chinese humans for a lack of morality and ethics, distancing the Chinese animalistic body from more proper, white society, and at other times focusing on their threatening, contaminating nature that demands removal from US soil. By uniting this range of negative traits under the straw man figure of "John Chinaman" and his rat-like embodiment, anti-Chinese rhetors were able to build a metonymic relationship between Chinese people and the threat of an Asian digestive capacity that would inevitably weaken the US's families, citizens, and workforce, eating the new nation from the inside out.

THE WAGES OF MASCULINITY

The imagined geography of Orientalism is one that "dramati[zes] the difference and distance between what is close to it and what is far away."[13] The fears surrounding Asian forms of embodiment and proximity to American citizens emerge from a belief that just as the US workforce is coequal with the national body, foreign geographies produce fundamentally different physiologies that labor differently. Proximity to the Chinese rat eater is therefore proximity to filth that might infect the white male worker, prompting a degrading transformation in his embodiment that in turn will threaten the growth of the young nation with an Asiatic kink. In an 1869 poem, Robert W. Hume warns the "sturdy" American workers that they are going to be "swarmed" by the locust-like Asian, and he directly details the changes this swarm might force upon the consumption habits of white laborers.

You sturdy tillers of the soil
Prepare to leave full soon;

---

13. Said, *Orientalism*, 55.

You'll find there is not room.
Like an Egyptian locust plague,
Or like an eastern blight,
He'll swarm you out of all your fields,
And seize them as his right.
Let the mechanics pack his traps, and ready make to flit;
He cannot live on rats and mice,
And so he needs must quit.[14]

At first, the Chinese worker is figured as a locust, an insect that is known for bringing famine to lands because of its unending appetite. Having "swarmed" the right/white workers out of the fields, the implication is that the environment is so changed that there is nothing left to eat besides rats and mice—a landscape of scarcity that would result in the starvation of white laborers. The white laborer cannot eat rats and mice because he does not have access to the "common sensations, concepts, images, ideas, attitudes" that allow the Chinese to sup on such vile creatures.[15] Perhaps even more disturbing is the implication that staying in such a landscape would fundamentally change the white worker's gut so that he could begin to stomach eating rodents; the "cannot live" statement is mayhap less focused on scarcity than on the presumed horrifying changes to his moral viewpoint that such changed consumption habits would evidence. Similar fears of the transformed white body, specifically in relation to eating practices, was part of the dominant discourse about Chinese joining the US workforce. After the prominent Cameron family hired Chinese workers to work in the Colorado mines, a white miner was quoted as saying, "Possibly the alarmists are right in professing to look forward with dismay to the prospect of our wearing pigtails and eating our rice and beans with chopsticks a few years hence."[16] The belief that close juxtaposition of different races would create unescapable influence on intimate acts like dressing and eating encapsulates the fear of increased proximity to the Chinese man as a threat to white masculine embodiment.

Dominant understandings of masculinity at this time coupled physical effort and financial reward as the conjoined measure of virtuous manhood. In European tradition, the ideal of the "Heroic Artisan" was a "physically powerful figure" that "represented self-employed, property-owning craftsmen and embodied the republican virtues of hard work, frugality, self-denial, and per-

---

14. Tchen, *New York before Chinatown,* 174.
15. Burke, *Rhetoric of Motives,* 21.
16. Wei, *Asians in Colorado,* 49.

sonal independence."[17] In this archetype, the careful maintenance of one's body and mind directly leads to a smoother working process and higher-quality product; one's commitment to an elevated moral and physical standard will emerge in and ensure success in one's labor. As the devastating uncertainty of events like the Gold Rush demonstrated the tenuousness of the link between diligent labor and economic success, leaving many white US citizens in financial ruin, it became more difficult to define white manhood in terms of this equation of self-betterment toward guaranteed financial gain. Michael Kimmel points out that "Westward expansion came to an abrupt end at the Pacific coast, and rapid industrialization radically altered men's relationships to their work. The independent artisan, the autonomous small farmer, and the small shopkeeper were everywhere disappearing."[18] The rapid corporatization of America abstracted the relationship of work, products, and customers, displacing agency and self-control away from the craftsman's immediate labor and physicality. The grunt work labor associated with these immigrant bodies also came to be "associated with a perverse temporality, one that rendered Chinese bodies fungible (like currency) and a signifier of moral corruption."[19] The rat-eating figure of "John Chinaman" is thus both an expression of existential anxieties about earning a living and an attempt to rhetorically bracket the increasing economic competition.

The need for cheap labor was in tension with the need to frame the US as a white, non-Asian country. Those who controlled American capital and commerce praised the value of Chinese immigrant labor; General Grenville Dodge praised the speed with which Chinese tracklayers worked and "found them eminently desirable as employees—'very quiet, handy, good cooks, and good at almost everything they are put at.'"[20] However, such positive descriptions masked how Chinese workers were usually paid "between one-half and two-thirds of what white workers cost."[21] Simultaneously, the white working class was scrambling for strategies to both disidentify with all Asian foreigners and reassert their superior cultural position. The Chinese male laborers' contribution to the workforce was not equal to white men's diligence but rather framed as an "almost inhuman adaptation to contemporary forms of modern labor" that revealed an underlying foreign embodiment.[22] The tension between the necessity of outside labor for Westward expansion and the socioeconomic

17. Currarino, "'Meat vs. Rice,'" 477.
18. Kimmel, *History of Men*, 63.
19. I. Day, *Alien Capital*, 76.
20. Bain, *Empire Express*, 640.
21. Chang and Fishkin, introduction, 2.
22. Hayot, *Hypothetical Mandarin*, 102.

threat of these immigrants is evident in the rhetorical erasure of much of this necessary work. In the epideictic events and texts related to the Transcontinental Railroad, the immense contribution of Chinese workers was glossed over. Although thousands of Chinese workers were crucial to the completion of the Central Pacific track, none were included in the photography of the final commemoration ceremony.[23] Similarly, in the famous painting of the golden spike ceremony *The Last Spike* by Thomas Hill, there are but two Chinese laborers in the foreground, a representation that hides how at times up to 90 percent of the workforce was Chinese immigrants.[24] The visualizations of US expansion do not reflect the extent to which Chinese labor was necessary for the completion of such projects and overall progress.

As the country and industry developed further, more business-class Chinese immigrated, exacerbating fears that US capitalism might not be the superior breed. Particularly, many of the Chinese who began restaurants in San Francisco in the mid-1800s were of the merchant class, primarily from Canton, who came "to develop trade and establish businesses such as boardinghouses, tool stores, herbal medical shops, or restaurants."[25] While the racial climate meant that Chinese men were often forced to work in restaurants owned by fellow immigrants, these new residents made the most of their new occupations. Once these businesses were established, the merchants brought over laborers and workers to staff these new sources of income, adding to the current residents' anxiety about ever-increasing competition. Several of the original Chinese-run restaurants in San Francisco, such as Canton Restaurant and Macao and Woosung Restaurant, were "larger in scale and more professional in operation than their Western counterparts at that time," including trendy bars and excellent waitstaff.[26] There also was a strong merchant presence in New York City as early as 1855, with these cigar makers and store owners earning "pay at least as good as that of sailors"—a highly dangerous job that required high economic incentives—by the 1870s.[27] As the presence of these businesses increased, the rhetoric of omission became more and more augmented by attention to this foreignness of body and mind, evidenced by these strange consumption habits.

The rhetorical emphasis on this suspicious metonymic connection between Chinese and vermin highlighted the status of the US as a nation on the cusp of greatness while also providing a convincing rationale for barring

23. Eng, *Racial Castration*, 36.
24. Chang, "The Chinese," 350.
25. Liu, *From Canton Restaurant*, 11.
26. Liu, *From Canton Restaurant*, 21.
27. Tchen, *New York before Chinatown*, 227.

Chinese competition from full inclusion in this economic development. A key part of this rhetorical problem was temporarily solved through framing Chinese labor as abstract and white labor as concrete. This separation renders Chinese laborers as "parasitic" burdens on "a concrete white labor host" who is elevated enough to seek self-actualized specificity.[28] Yet despite occupying a morally superior position, the white worker might still become a victim of "quantity over quality, of consistent small effort over large heroic ones, of the faceless horde over the individual, and of mass production over unalienated, organic labor."[29] This forging of associations with nonhuman labor and Chinese embodiment provided anti-Chinese rhetors with evidence for exclusion on both an interpersonal and a national level. Not only were Chinese men rat eaters, introducing vileness into their own bodies, they were also rat-like carriers of moral disease, spreading a weakening contagion that would irrevocably alter the capacities of white male workers and the growth of the US economy.

JOHN CHINAMAN'S DIET

As Homi Bhabha argues, the "construction of colonial discourse is then a complex articulation of the tropes of fetishism—metaphor and metonymy— and the forms of narcissistic and aggressive identification available to the Imaginary."[30] The metonymical relationship between Chinese and rats offered a form of rhetorical disidentification that centered Western racial purity as natural by posing an imaginary, yet convincing, opposite whose slavering jaws needed to be held at arm's length. From within such a perspective of interracial rivalries, discriminatory hiring and immigration practices are not racist exclusions but necessary means to protect the health of the workers and nation from contamination. The xenophobic projections of Chinese men as violently deviant eaters, as seen in the folk character of "John Chinaman," work to rhetorically limn Asian forms of consumption, and thus embodiment, as fundamentally illegible from within a Western sphere. Throughout this period, anti-Chinese rhetors were able to leverage this link between illegible eating and strange ontologies to argue for exclusionary legislation and social practices as prophylactic measures.

The rhetorical formation of John Chinaman as the emblematic inscrutable eater was crucial to arguments for increased racial separation. Jerry Won Lee

28. I. Day, *Alien Capital*, 62.
29. Hayot, *Hypothetical Mandarin*, 103.
30. Bhabha, *Location of Culture*, 110.

argues that "the figure of the so-called Oriental, rather than inscrutable *as such,* is *rendered as* inscrutable through the gaze or perspective of the Westerner who is unable to or refuses to read the Oriental."[31] In the nineteenth-century American discourse on race, labor, and consumption, this construction of an inscrutable gut via John Chinaman posits these deviant diets as indicative of Asian bodies' illegibility in relation to Western standards. The word "diet" "comes from the Greek *dieta,* which means 'regimen' or, more broadly, 'way of life.' Therefore, subjectivity and ingestivity have been tied together as a solution to the problem of democratic citizenship."[32] Diets, or ways of consuming, are effective rhetorical levers for debates around in-group belonging because they index fears and anxieties about the validity about one's chosen way of life and the available paths for "acting-together" with one's neighbors.[33] As the evidence for the upward mobility of Chinese labor grew, diet "became one of the arenas of struggle over racial superiority" and one of the main rhetorical battlegrounds for defining US identity in opposition to an Asian upstart.[34] While racialized femininity is often posed as that which is to be metaphorically and sexually consumed, here, Oriental masculinity is presumed to be that which consumes wrongly.

The figuring of Chinese identity as coterminous with a range of rat-like characteristics was used to rhetorically depict a homogenous swarm of Asian invaders who would fundamentally degrade the character of American life. Common visuals of the time regularly portrayed the Chinese as rat-like, with descriptions of their wretched living conditions and illustrations of their long hair as active, prehensile tails. Even more explicitly, Johannes Keppler, the founder of *Puck* magazine, illustrated a set of images, titled "The Chinese Invasion," portraying Chinese immigrants as the latest wave of "invading" foreigners to the US. As the Chinese swim toward the outstretched arms of Lady Liberty, they transform from rat-shaped figures, tails wriggling in the surf, to humans. Although Keppler saw the Chinese as potentially part of the US landscape, his portrayal still relies on an assumption of needed removal of the rat-like qualities from their persons before they could become productive members of American society. By 1880, this stereotype was common enough that the Cigar Maker's International Union promised "first class workmanship" from its members as opposed to the "tenement house, Prison, Chinese and rat-shop workmanship."[35]

---

31. J. Lee, *Politics of Translingualism,* 56.
32. DuPuis, *Dangerous Digestion,* 5–6.
33. Burke, *Rhetoric of Motives,* 21.
34. DuPuis, *Dangerous Digestion,* 70. See also Elias, "Palate of Power."
35. Shah, *Contagious Divides,* 163.

In depictions of rats as the primary source of nourishment for Chinese workers, the merging of Chinese and rat bodies through eating creates a "form of bizarre bodily intimacy" between them.[36] The specter of uncivilized cravings that produce warped bodies is exemplified in an advertisement for "Rough on Rats" pesticide from the E. S. Wells Trade Company. The image portrays a Chinese man in traditional dress with a long queue, mouth open and ready to bite into a rat. He holds another in his left hand. Atop the advertisement is the corpse of a rat, stretched out on its back. A banner frames the Chinese man, reading "It Clears Out. They Must Go" across his head, and then on either side lists several of the things this poison works on, including rats, mice, bedbugs (left banner), and flies and roaches (right banner). The "They" of the banner is purposefully multitasking, indicating that Chinese and the rats both "must go," widening the gap of possible identification between the presumably white viewer and the Chinese "rat eater." This slippage between rat and human operates within the "metonymic topographies" that "animate recognition" of queer resonances between the Chinese body and the rat's.[37] The Chinese man's body is that which seeks out and invites in the filth of rats voluntarily.

This visualization of Chinese men eating rats creates a visual template in which rats and Asianness are naturally bound together. The capacities of Asian embodiment are unambiguously closer to the animal than the human. The encouragement to match Chinese embodiment and rat eating was a common trope during this period. A Protestant missionary, E. R. Donehoo, recalled being shown a lantern slideshow in which "there emerged from the gloom a monster rat, whereupon the Chinaman opened his capacious jaws, and the rat aforesaid made a wild plunge down his throat. Soon another rat appeared and disappeared in like manner, and another, and still another."[38] Just as in the "Rough on Rats" advertisement, this bit of children's entertainment portrayed the eating of rats not as a matter of cultural difference or even survival but as an uncontrollable delirium of consumption.

This metonymic link between Asian males and rat-like eating casts them as fundamentally flawed at the level of food-based desires, which in turn casts a shadow over Asian subjectivity more broadly. Metonymies in particular rely on amorphous substitutions in which "the object that functions as a metonym for something else may carry meanings and implications beyond the object itself."[39] The creation and use of metonyms is thus an operation of interpretation and attribution, which means they are fertile rhetorical ground for fixing

36. M. Chen, *Animacies*, 111.
37. King, "Hitching Wagons," 86.
38. Tchen, *New York before Chinatown*, 273.
39. Goehring, Renegar, and Puhl, "'Abusive Furniture,'" 444.

FIGURE 1. "Rough on Rats" advertisement. Courtesy of
Chinese Historical Society of America, circa 1900.

moral implications to an otherwise neutral object. For example, "associations
between whiteness and innocence, for example, are metonymic," rather than
natural, but the repetition over time has become enfranchised in ways that
shape commonly accepted understandings of racial inherency.[40] In the case of
Asian men and rats, the establishment of this metonymic link provided tenable rationales for accusing them of a range of disconnected, yet all morally
suspect, behaviors.

The indexical relationship that formed between Chinese male bodies, rats,
and rat eating is one in which the Chinese man is always shadowed by vermin,

40. King, "Hitching Wagons," 85.

which means that physical closeness to such a body is also closeness to the accompanying rat's taint. The prevalence and popularity of Chinese restaurants during the Gold Rush and beyond exposed a great number of people to the deliciousness of Chinese cuisine, but this visible copresence of Asianness and strange food also provided fertile ground for forging metonymic links between Asianness and deviant forms of consumption. Originally, the gold miners liked Chinese food because it was tasty and cheap. Gold miner William Shaw is quoted as saying, "The best eating houses in San Francisco are those kept by Celestials and conducted in Chinese fashion," and James Ayer's diary claimed, "The best restaurants—at least that was my experience—were kept by Chinese and the poorest and dearest by Americans."[41] Even so, the "exotic" appeal lent even the beloved chop suey a note of suspicion; restaurant guides of the time recommended that diners "not ask too much about the ingredients."[42]

These mostly positive descriptions of the "chow-chow, curry, and tarts" found at Chinese restaurants were eventually replaced by dominant suspicions of deviant eating.[43] The *Daily Alta California* newspaper was originally favorably disposed toward Chinese immigrants, but later articles began to uptake the negative views of Chinese food, with one editorial deeming a Chinese restaurant a "Chinese roast-a-rat."[44] Another defined the Chinese diet as "rats, lizards, mud-terrapins, [and] rank and indigestible shell-fish" that would "turn the stomachs of the stoutest Anglo-Saxon."[45] In a popular textbook, *The Child's Second Book of History,* US schoolchildren were taught that "many parts of China is [sic] so thickly settled, that nothing which will support life is thrown away. Puppies, rats and mice are constantly hawked about the streets for sale."[46] A news report from New York's the *Daily Graphic* in 1879 described a gambling den as "one of the places which are popularly supposed to abound in pickled rat, edible dog and savory candles, but whose main source of income is really derived from the lucrative but forbidden opium traffic."[47] The author Mark Twain recounts a Chinese shopkeeper offering him sausages "of which we could have swallowed several yards if we had chosen to try, but we suspected that each link contained the corpse of a mouse, and

41. Liu, *From Canton Restaurant,* 20.
42. Gabaccia, *We Are What We Eat,* 104.
43. Liu, *From Canton Restaurant,* 22.
44. Hannis, "Comparative Analysis," 262.
45. Hannis, "Comparative Analysis," 265.
46. Tchen, *New York before Chinatown,* 265.
47. Tchen, *New York before Chinatown,* 263.

therefore refrained."[48] The Chinese form of consumption is gradually painted as not only vile but as linked to increasingly deceptive behaviors and practices, from gambling to food adulteration. The deliciousness of Chinese food is rhetorically formulated as an alluring trap that masks its Asiatic harm to both bodies and economic systems.

FIXING ASIAN MANHOOD

The repeated visualizations of Chinese bodies living in a rat-like manner, greedily and without compunction, set up and maintained a metonymical relationship between rat flesh and contamination that permanently restricts the Asian body's access to manhood. Cathryn Bailey points out how racist "somatophobic arguments," such as the idea that African Americans are more impervious to pain than whites, "have rested upon the view that animals were different in kind and subordinate to human beings," and the "logical next step, then, was to offer arguments and evidence that various other groups were either closer to animals or within the category itself."[49] In the many texts that focus on John Chinaman, the eating of rats is used to frame him as someone who is repeatedly offered the chance to assimilate to US values and yet refuses. The disgusting behaviors such as rat and puppy eating are accompanied by his unwillingness to give up the physical marker that is analogous with rats and the wrong sort of gendered performance: his queue. A common minstrel song simply titled "John Chinaman" clearly lays out a consuming binary between the welcoming, clean American and the contaminated, consuming Chinese body that resists needed alteration.

John Chinaman, John Chinaman
But five short years ago,
I welcomed you from Canton, John—
But wish I hadn't though
For then I thought you honest, John,
Not dreaming but you'd make
A citizen as useful, John
As any in the state.

I thought you'd open wide your ports
And let our merchants in

---

48. Twain, *Roughing It*, 323.
49. Bailey, "We Are What We Eat," 42.

To barter for their crepes and teas
Their wares of wood and tin.

I thought you'd cut your queue off, John,
And don a Yankee coat,
And a collar high you'd raise, John,
Around your dusky throat.
I imagined that the truth, John,
You'd speak when under oath,
But I find you'll lie and steal too—
Yes John you're up to both.

I thought of rats and puppies, John,
You'd eaten your last fill;
But on such slimy pot-pies, John,
I'm told you dinner still.

Oh, John, I've been deceived in you,
And all your thieving clan,
For our gold is all you're after, John,
To get it as you can[50]

The speaker, positioned as a white American citizen, begins as a welcoming figure, assuming that "John" holds the acceptable desire of assimilation
and citizenship. Instead, "John" takes advantage of his American hosts, all
the while maintaining hygiene and consumption practices that offend on an
equal level as "lying and stealing." To assimilate correctly, John is supposed
to remove or mask as many signs of his foreign origin as possible, from cutting off his queue to hiding his "dusky throat." The desired transformation of
the appearance of the Chinese body equates removing the tendency toward
predation on rats and puppies with removing overt signs of race and gender. The queue, as a sign of the "sexually ambiguous" nature of Chinese manhood, must be permanently removed.[51] Without these changes, John cannot be
allowed full inclusion into the civilized Western sphere as a "useful" citizen.

John's digestive inclinations are also metonymically tied to his ethical
capabilities, as seen in the continued eating of rats and puppies. Jennifer
Moon points out how interracial distinctiveness was based on common views
of racial diets. While the racist view of African Americans as violent was sup-

50. Wallach and Swindall, *American Appetites*, 71–72.
51. Ou, "Chinese Ethnicity," 67.

ported by their catching and eating of forest animals like raccoons and pos-
sums, the link between Asian populations and small animals like "vermin,
which were abundant in cities, [and] were easily caught," signals the difference between the masculine Western hunter and the Chinese scavenger.[52] The
Asian male can then be critiqued upon two axes, for both the strangeness
and the effeminacy of his appetites. Immediately following this denigration
of Asian-style consumption, the narrator renders an ethical judgment—"I've
been deceived in you"—and attributes John's treachery as his belonging to a
larger "thieving clan." Just as rat eating is a signal of a nonmasculine embodiment, thievery is a signal of the always deceptive Chinese embodiment. The
listeners and viewers needed to be aware that there was a risk of contamination, not from merely touching or smelling the Chinese, but from adopting
consumption practices that could tint a white body yellow in terms of ethics
and morality.

The continued reperformance of this metonymic link between Chinese
people and either eating or being rats affirms the rightness of a distant proximity between whites and Asians, particularly in terms of appropriate gender
performance. Just as the characters of "Zip Coon" and "Jim Crow" were racial
straw *men* that allowed white audiences to assume a superior identity and
legitimate distance between racialized performances of gender, the yellowface
character "John Chinaman" enabled a continued understanding of Asian men
as "fundamentally foreign" through calling attention to "differences such as
religious practices, eating habits, and English proficiency."[53] In particular, the
continued association of Chinese food with rats, dogs, and opium worked
to rhetorically reinscribe the inferiority of Chinese bodies and performance
of masculinity. Importantly, this was not just a lack of success in romance
but a signal of deeper, fundamental wrongness of gender. The simultaneous
copresence of these masculine and feminine characteristics renders the Chinese body a sort of "mutilated" male that evokes disgust for its wrongness.[54]
In the context of colonial South Africa, accusers used the queue as evidence
of Chinese laborers performing male prostitution; the "way he does his hair
up" is presented as a given sign of homosexuality.[55] The queue comes to stand
for wrongness of gender, sexuality, and gut-level embodiment in a way that is
not assimilable into Western society.

The rhetorical emphasis on this wrongness of embodiment supports the
framing of racial violence as the cleansing of a contaminated area, rather than

---

52. Moon, *Yellowface*, 48.
53. Moon, *Yellowface*, 32.
54. Dolmage, "Metis, Mêtis."
55. Bright, "Migration, Masculinity," 573.

as terrorism of minority communities. At the time, the regular practice of violently removing Chinese men's queues was framed in terms analogous to castrating feral animals.[56] Charles DeLong, a lawyer and Democratic politician, wrote in his diary about "collecting" the braided hair of Chinamen. In an entry from 1929, he described the violent act of tracking down Chinese men and cutting off their hair as an evening of pranks and tomfoolery: "Supper at Hesse's Crossing went down the river in the night collected all the way had a great time, Chinamen tails cut off," much as a farmer might dock a cow's tail.[57] Of course, the violence often extended beyond merely cutting off the Chinese men's hair. During the Denver race riot of 1880, white members of the mob cut off the "cue" of a young Chinese man, Look Young, before beating him to death and destroying the majority of the businesses in Chinatown.[58] These acts of violence "allowed white men in the mid and late nineteenth century to reenact, at least at a symbolic level, an earlier savage eighteenth-century ritual—scalping."[59] In various British colonies such as Australia and South Africa, there were regular reports of physical violence that ranged from pulling on Chinese men's braids, cutting the queues off, or using them as rope for attempting lynchings.[60] Yet the overt violence of such actions is minimized through the association of the queues with "tails," which in the context of the references to animality, connotes "fixing" the Chinese male body in multiple senses of the term.

Such violations were not isolated incidents of violent misunderstanding but fit into a broader pattern of framing Chinese male embodiment as that which needs forcible correction. In the case of the "Queue Ordinances" of 1878 in San Francisco, it was mandated that all prisoners have their hair shaved within an inch of their scalp, regardless of race. In response, a lawsuit brought forth by Ho Ah Kow directly called out how this ordinance targeted Chinese males in particular, noting that had "the ordinance contemplated a mere sanitary regulation it would have been limited to such cases and made applicable to females as well as to males, and to persons awaiting trial as well as to persons under conviction."[61] The lawsuit states directly that the removal of a Chinese man's queue leads to "disgrace among his countrymen, and carries with

---

56. See Flores, *Deportable and Disposable* for descriptions of this form of assault against brown bodies, specifically Mexican American zoot suiters, in the 1940s. In addition to forcibly stripping zoot suiters of their clothing, military gangs purposefully went after the "Argentine duck-tail" haircut, removing it during the violent assaults.

57. R. Lee, *Orientals*, 40.

58. Wei, *Asians in Colorado*, 132.

59. R. Lee, *Orientals*, 40.

60. Bright, "Migration, Masculinity," 570.

61. Cooley, "Ho Ah Kow," 678.

it the constant dread of misfortune and suffering after death."[62] These removals are not aimed at allowing the Chinese male body to continue existing as such but rather at mutilating the racial/gendered elements so they are beyond repair. The threat of making someone a cultural eunuch is insidious indeed, with a sort of half-life as the maximum achievement possible. Yet even the removal of the queue was understood as not installing Chinese masculinity as equal with white Americanness. Rather, the rat-like appetites that will destroy the nascent nation move throughout the Chinese body, sometimes evident in the queue but other times in behavior of the gut.

CONSUMING AMERICA'S FUTURE

The vernacular texts and childhood songs examined thus far wove the metonymic linkage between Chinese men and rats into the fabric of US discourse on race. The segregation that led to the creation of Chinatowns, ghettos that kept these eaters mostly away from view when they were not working in the kitchens or laundries for wealthy white households, reflects a fear that the Chinese appetites are so indiscriminate as to destroy the burgeoning nation. Lisa Flores points out how the discourse surrounding the Mexican immigrant operates via "an easy conflation of criminality and undocumented entry" where the end goal of deportation is taken as evidence for the immigrant's a priori corruption.[63] Similarly, the supposed need to expel the rat-like Asian male from polite society was rhetorically leveraged as a sign of the inherent toxicity of Asian labor. These understandings of Asianness as rat-like were oppositional "embodiable topoi that shaped common sense about the body of the national public," specifically as direct threats to the vulnerable, post–Civil War nation.[64] The posing of Asian bodies as rat-like in terms of indiscriminate devouring enables the rhetorical framing of Asian eating as not just rapacious but also ethically inferior; it is not just that the Asian eater eats so much but that they do not *discriminate* in ways that align with an ethically elevated American identity. Picky eating, in this case, is a sign of ethics that scales upward to a strong, curated national workforce.

The political cartoon titled "The Problem Solved" visualizes the threat of Asian consuming power as that which, due to its new proximity to the US nation, is a ravenous threat to the American way of life. In the three-panel cartoon, an Irish man and Chinese man are both in the process of consum-

---

62. Cooley, "Ho Ah Kow," 680.
63. Flores, *Deportable and Disposable*, 39.
64. Olson, "Performing Embodiable Topoi," 314.

ing Uncle Sam, the Irish man starting at the head and the Chinese man at the feet. After they jointly work to polish off Uncle Sam, the Chinese man then betrays his fellow diner and swallows the Irish man whole. The top panel caption reads, "The great fear of the period that Uncle Sam may be Swallowed by foreigners," and the bottom caption reads, "The problem solved."[65] Similar to most satirical cartoons of the time, both the Irish man and the Chinese man bear exaggerated racial features: The Irish man's prominent brow bone and unkempt hair are posed opposite the Chinese man's pointed queue and eyes so slanted as to appear closed. The Irish man is depicted as slovenly via a hobo's bindle, and the coolie hat of a farmer rests by the Chinese man's feet.

Although both characters are portrayed as outsiders who resort to cannibalism, it is the Chinese body that is portrayed as so voracious in its bodily appetites as to eat its own ally. As with the "Rough on Rats" image, the Chinese man straddles the link between man and animal. While the Irish man's hands are closed into proper fists and rest on Uncle Sam's arms, balancing Sam's body rather than clutching at it, the Chinese man's fingers point upward, grasping at his victim's flesh like talons, eagerly pushing the flesh of Uncle Sam into his mouth. The two figures are portrayed as roughly equal in size, and they begin the first panel eating roughly the same amount of Uncle Sam. Yet the eating power of the Chinese man is quickly shown in the second panel, where the Irish man is still struggling with Uncle Sam's head, but the Chinese man is already past Sam's knees. Notably, in all three panels, the Chinese man's feet are portrayed as in mid-stride, while the Irish man's feet are planted as if resisting a great wave of force. The Chinese figure, in its never-ceasing forward movement, steadily advances through Uncle Sam's body/across the US in a sort of mockery of Westward expansion and Manifest Destiny, consuming rather than surveying as he heads to the West Coast.

After swallowing the Irish man, the Chinese man is still in his same traditional dress but now is visibly enlarged, rendered more looming over the North American landscape via the eating of both Uncle Sam and the Irish man. His queue, still neatly braided and tied, now sticks up in a more vertical, phallus-like position, pushed more erect after donning the Irishman's stolen hat. This slovenly drag demonstrates how Asian desires are destructive in both the short and the long term; not only does he consume his only ally in the US, but he also cannot even convincingly assimilate once he has done

---

65. See Roediger, *How Race Survived* for details on how both Irish and Chinese immigrants during this time were portrayed as outside the bounds of whiteness. Ironically enough, as anti-Chinese legislation prevented the immigration of Chinese women, many Chinese men ended up marrying Irish women.

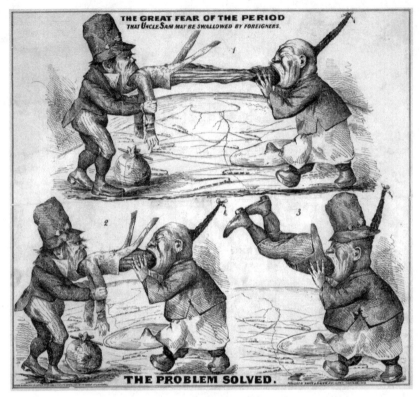

FIGURE 2. "The great fear of the period that Uncle Sam may be swallowed by foreigners: the problem solved." Library of Congress, 1860–69.

so. This cartoon exemplifies the feared threat of transforming on a gut level, a transformation that skews both stomachs and morals.

Labor activists, struggling to achieve fairer working conditions and wages against the might of industrial titans, took up this rhetoric of immoral taste explicitly. As is clear throughout the famed and oft-cited pamphlet "Some Reasons for Chinese Exclusion. Meat vs. Rice. American Manhood against Asiatic Coolieism. Which Shall Survive?," forms of eating and living were persuasive evidence for how the Asian laborer who eats poorly must also labor poorly. Samuel Gompers, then president of the AFL, and Herman Gutstadt, a prominent member, wrote this pamphlet to argue that the US government should extend the Chinese Exclusion Act of 1882 and stop further Asian immigration. Early on, they compare the supposed problem of Chinese immigration with the new wave of Japanese laborers, arguing that the lack of a Japanese Exclusion Act has led to these immigrants "com[ing] in swarms, like bees, until the high water mark was reached in 1907, 30,226 being admitted that year, or about 9,000 less than the Chinese emigration of 1882 (39,579), which caused the great Kearney riots and almost led to the destruction of the Pacific Mail Docks."[66] The continued presence of these different animalistic ontologies will lead to an impotent white labor force, and therefore distancing action must be taken to preserve the upward mobility of workers and this young nation.[67]

The Chinese-as-vermin linkage enables Gompers and Gutstadt to reaffirm white American workers' place at the top of the racial working hierarchy through defining Western standards for daily living in direct opposition to the Asiatic abnormality. The "meat vs. rice" phrase of the title is quoted from a speech given in 1879 by James G. Blaine, a congressman and secretary of state, where he declares that it would be disastrous for Americans to attempt to convert or assimilate the Chinese because doing so would not "bring up the man who lives on rice to the beef-and-bread standard, but to bring down the beef-and-bread man to the rice standard." This oft-cited quote poses dietary practices as evidence of the Chinese body contaminating and then weakening the virility of the American male. Racial differences can be felt on the level of the gut's desires and permanently impact the regenerative properties of the individual nuclear family and the nation. The ability of the Chinese body to live amidst scarcity is a warning sign of the future instability of the labor climate.

For many formerly destitute European Americans, beef and the ability to eat it multiple times a week signaled the prosperous opportunities of the new nation.[68] The superiority of the US as a nation was directly linked to both a "rejection of foreign products and excess" and the "'American right' to consume rich foods."[69] In contrast, the prominent Chinese restaurant culture during the Gold Rush featured dishes of primarily vegetables, leading to an understanding of Chinese people as those "who ate less meat."[70] Rather than being viewed as a matter of culinary preference or economic background, the lack of desire for Angus steaks was construed as a key piece of evidence for the Chinese man's lack of virility, impugning both his individual bodily prowess and his capacity to create new generations of strong Americans. To put it

---

66. Gompers and Gutstadt, "Some Reasons," 3–4.

67. In "The Chinese Question" by Edwin Meade, he also uses an apidaen metaphor, claiming that from "their Asiatic hive they still come pouring forth, and it is fair to presume, will increase in volume as the advantages of the outside world in wages and liberal government become better known" (5). In the 1901 version of "Meat vs. Rice," the frontispiece is an illustration of a European American laborer, tied to the floor with banners that read "Cheap Labor" by several tiny Chinese figures, titled "The American Gulliver and the Chinese Lilliputians." The threat of the multiplied, drone-like Chinese body is clear.

68. Specht, *Red Meat Republic.*

69. Councilor, "Feeding the Body," 145.

70. DuPuis, *Dangerous Digestion,* 54.

bluntly, "in a sexist society that symbolizes woman as meat, as a sexually consumable object, the man who declines to eat [her] is effectively announcing his failure as a heterosexual."[71] The presumed absence of livestock meat-eating, coupled with the presumed desire for rat flesh, became a specter upon which Americans could project their racial anxieties and build a negative imaginary of Oriental desires that not only failed to meet the standards of white male masculinity but that also threatened the integrity of national standards for patriotic labor and consumerism. Besides the embedded racism, such rhetoric also "mixed real issues of poverty—places where people were so poor they supposedly only eat rice—with ideas of national worker deservedness."[72]

The focus on diet directly impacting one's work output enables a reclamation of the presumed elevated moral state of white men despite their threatened financial position while casting Asian workers as those that will smuggle in "indigestion" to the US body politic. In an attempt to forestall such accusations and associated violence, Chinese community leaders purposefully framed their involvement in the US economic system as temporary and leaving no trace. In her memoirs, Caroline C. Leighton recounts an "Address to the Public" in which Chinese leaders explained that "We lift others up" and "The money that you pay us for our labor, we send home; but the work remains for you."[73] Despite this apparent acceptance of their demeaned position in the US social hierarchy, this abasement was used as evidence of Chinese masculinity's selfishness and permanent outsider status in laments like "[the Chinese] come for employment and for gain, with expectation for the most part of returning to enjoy their acquisitions in their native homes."[74] Refusing to accumulate goods, households, and goods for those households is viewed as not just a lack of participation but an act of quiet sabotage to the national economy. In his later 1893 speech "What Does Labor Want?," Gompers clarifies that in addition to fairer labor conditions, the role of the trade unions is to "give the great body of people more time, more opportunity and more leisure in order to create and increase their consumptive power; in other words, to relieve the choked and glutted condition of industry and commerce." The displacement of white workers is not a problem solely because of race but because such a displacement so warps the proper ratio of American production and consumption; the Chinese "seemed *too* good at living American virtues of frugality, self-denial, and thrift," to the point where their self-control is a threat to the consumption/labor relationship.[75]

71. Bailey, "We Are What We Eat," 44–45.
72. DuPuis, *Dangerous Digestion*, 71.
73. Leighten, *Life at Puget Sound*, 229.
74. H. Day, "Chinese Migration," 6.
75. Currarino, "'Meat vs. Rice,'" 483.

This apparent lack of appropriate consumptive desire was paired with suspicion of the lack of heteronormative marriages and families in Chinese communities. Gompers and Gutstadt quote John P. Irish's testimony that the employment of Chinese "is generally in droves," and the workmen "live in sheds or in strawstacks, do their own cooking, have no homes, and are without interest in their work or the country. The white laborer who would compete with them must not only pursue the same kind of life but must, like them, abdicate his individuality."[76] The result of such wrongly feminized living would be "a laboring class without homes, without families, and without any of the restraining influences of society."[77] Although the focus of this passage is supposedly on the increased financial insecurity of white laborers, the language used focuses on the potential changes to white ontologies. The "droves" of rat-like Chinese not only fail at masculinity, "do[ing] their own cooking," but they also "abdicate" human qualities like living in real homes because of their lack of "interest." Mel Chen points out that such hierarchies are deeply rhetorical, using groupings as a prejudiced "*generativity*, mapping and marking reproductive and nonreproductive bodies" in opposition.[78] Eating and working in the manner of a Chinese is to live in animalistic abandon, spawning decidedly nonheteronormative, possibly miscegenative family trees. Karen Leong argues that such enthymematic reasoning helped maintain an understanding of Chinese gender relations as warped and thus all Chinese individuals as beyond the reach of US citizenship; "without a family, a 'Chinaman' had no reason to invest in the future well-being of the nation; without a wife, a 'Chinaman' was simply barbaric and uncivilized."[79] The Chinese choose to produce wrongly.[80]

It is not just that the Chinese refuse heteronormative relationships. Gompers and Gutstadt argue that the inevitable result of allowing the Chinese worker to continue living in such a way "underbids white labor and ruthlessly takes its place and will go on doing so until all the white laborers come down to the scanty food and half civilized habits of the Chinaman."[81] This

76. Gompers and Gutstadt, "Some Reasons," 15.

77. Gompers and Gutstadt, "Some Reasons," 15.

78. M. Chen, *Animacies*, 127.

79. Leong, "A Distinct," 114.

80. See Mink, *Old Labor*, 86 for a speech given at an anti-Chinese rally put on by the Workingmen's Party of California that argued, "If clover and hay be planted on the same soil, the clover will ruin the hay, because clover lives upon less than the hay, and so it is in this struggle between the races. The Mongolian race will live and run the Caucasian race out." This agricultural metaphor orients listeners toward ways of living and working that echo the values encapsulated in the "Heroic Artisan" figure and away from the abundance of dross that marks the Chinese. The listener is assumed to understand that because hay is a superior product to clover, a more nutritional feed for livestock, its slower growing time demonstrates its higher inherent worth.

81. Gompers and Gutstadt, "Some Reasons," 13.

results in a dystopic future where the "white laboring man" is "injured in his comfort, reduced in his scale of life and standard of living, necessarily carrying down with it his moral and physical stamina."[82] The main focus on the material issue of job competition and loss is framed as initiating a change in the bodies of white laborers, who will "come down to the scanty food and half civilized habits" of their competitors. Although this "coming down" could merely be a reference to reduced economic prospects, the successive framing of injury and reduction, "carrying down with it his moral and physical stamina," shifts the emphasis from the strictly material to the realm of the white laborers' bodily fortitude. The closing quote from the committee is even more emphatic, directly stating that the "greatness of a nation does not lie in its money, but in its men and women; and not in their number, but in their quality, in their virtue, honor, integrity, truth, and, above all things, in their courage and manhood."[83] The bodily labor that once marked the Heroic Artisan is held up as the ideal for civic virtue, and the rat-like Asian body threatens to degrade the white laborer's capacity to fulfill his duty as a fully participating consumer citizen.

Within these descriptions, the focus on inherent motivations diverts attention from the structural issues that directly led to a lack of heterosexual female partners for Chinese immigrants. For example, because of the Page Act of 1875, many Chinese men lived communally with other "bachelors" due to the barriers either to bringing their existing family to the US or to forming a new one. This belief that all Chinese women were prostitutes was, of course, a rhetorical fiction aimed at increasing distance from Chinese bodies. Even though many of the Chinese women who had managed to immigrate to the US had to work many menial jobs in addition to prostitution, such as piecework sewing for factories, they were solely described and regarded as prostitutes.[84] Yet the high number of "predominantly male communities suggested a moral inability to form and sustain families, a clear contrast with the heteronormativity of American society."[85] Fears of miscegenation with white women, the same that often arise with any marginalized community, further spurred the denigration of these men.

A news investigation of an alleged opium den in 1873 explicitly framed the connection between rat-like Asian eating and sexual predation that threatened white heteronormativity.

---

82. Gompers and Gutstadt, "Some Reasons," 13.
83. Gompers and Gutstadt, "Some Reasons," 14.
84. Shah, *Contagious Divides*, 81.
85. Leong, *China Mystique*, 10.

The investigation found "a handsome but squalidly dressed white girl." Interviewed about the girl's presence, the owner supposedly "replied with a horrible leer, Oh, hard time in New York. Young girl hungry. Plenty come here. Chinaman always want something to eat, and he like young white girl. He! He!"[86]

Here, the sexual predation and implied cannibalism work to reinforce each other's role as a marker of deviant embodiment that directly threatens white heteronormative relations. The Asian man is overtly feminine in his lack of mastery over the English language, signaled by the reproduction of a high pitched "He," yet his gleeful preying on a young, vulnerable girl signals the threat of such warped masculinity.

By focusing on the depraved manners of consumption, production, and family-making as entangled within Chinese male embodiment, anti-Chinese rhetors were able to refocus the question of job competition away from the shifting American market and toward the issue of this outsider morality that cannot be reconciled. The ideal of the multicultural American body politic quietly assumed that some racial groups "would pass through the nation's bowels undigested, unincorporated, and unchanged."[87] The Chinese male body is immune to assimilation to American life, evidenced by the strange embodiment that is so firmly attached to its prior habituation, developed on foreign soil and continued in dens of opium-laced iniquity. The desire to wallow in such habits means that the Chinese man only adapts to clean society when "it is in his interest to do so," and his true nature is to "joyfully hasten back to his slum and burrow, to the grateful luxury of his normal surroundings— vice, filth, and an atmosphere of horror."[88] Gompers and Gutstadt sum up the issue of Chinese social habits with a rhetorical question: "If, then, Asiatics are satisfied to live such a life and practice such habits—in a country where they are favored so financially—what must be their actual condition when less favored?"[89] The implication is clear; since Chinese immigrants cannot find it in themselves to change their consumption habits within the context of the American dream, their base embodiment must be so flawed, whether through habit or biology, as to permanently be beyond the limits of cultural or legal citizenship.

---

86. Cheung, "Anxious and Ambivalent," 299.
87. Councilor, "Feeding the Body," 150.
88. Gompers and Gutstadt, "Some Reasons," 17.
89. Gompers and Gutstadt, "Some Reasons," 17.

CONCLUSIONS

Regardless of the actual hygienic properties of Asian bodies in the late nineteenth century, the rhetorical messaging was overwhelmingly centered on their capacity to contaminate white spaces and existing forms of US labor. And indeed, these historical messages "profoundly influenced the subsequent creation and production of Asian American representation throughout the twentieth century as pollutants, enemy aliens, gooks, and model minorities, all of which express the nation's rejection or acceptance of its Asian American citizens based on cultural constructions of impropriety."[90] The framing of Asian bodies as those that actively pursue contaminated forms of consumption enabled a clear separation between "us" and "them" that allowed for the use of them as cheap labor as long as they were properly disposed of afterward. The ability to survive inhospitable environments and overcome poverty, seemingly the most American of ideals, is instead framed as evidence of inscrutable embodiment.

This assumed inscrutability enables rhetorics that proclaim bodies thick with contamination, spreading disease through mere proximity. A report from the Board of the City and County of San Francisco tells its reader to imagine a basement of a typical Chinatown building that is "thick with smoke and fetid with an indescribable odor of reeking vapors" that "the opium smoker sucks through his pipe bowl into his trained lungs." Amidst this malodorous reek that "is tangible to the sight, tangible to the touch, tangible to the taste, and, oh, how tangible to the smell," the Chinese people sleep "in this poisonous atmosphere until morning, proof against the baneful effects of the carbonic acid gas generated by this human defiance of chemical laws, and proof against all the zymotic poisons that would be fatal to a person of any other race."[91] The metaphoric language is used to evoke socially approved levels of sensory response to the perceived negative moral qualities of these hovels, "instantly evok[ing] a spectrum of temporal experiences via imagery," naturalizing aversion toward the Chinese and their associates on an affectively instinctual level.[92] If Chinese bodies not only thrive in but *leak* miasmic effluvia, the need to increase proximity between white Americans and Asian bodies becomes all the more exigent. Just as rats can adapt to cramped and fetid spaces, Chinese must be peculiarly able to inure their bodies to substances that would be "fatal" to members of all other races by funneling their secreted toxins into the local environment.

---

90. Chiu, *Filthy Fictions*, 8.
91. Gompers and Gutstadt, "Some Reasons," 16.
92. LeMesurier, "Somatic Metaphors," 371.

The case of labeling male Chinese workers as "rat eaters" illuminates how Asian racialization is not merely a by-product of a "foundational anti-blackness" but instead part of a more complicated organization of expected distances between races based on fictionalized ontologies that crave filth.[93] Although the primary purpose of forging an understanding of Chinese men as failures of both race and gender was to support arguments against Chinese immigration, defining racial belonging as grounded in distinct forms of consumption and emission also forwards a necessary level of separation between differently racialized bodies. It is not just that the Chinese ate strange objects (as historian Vincent J. Cannato points out, early Italian immigrants were derided as "spaghetti benders" and "garlic eaters") but that their presumed ways of eating—predatory, nondiscerning, and rapacious—exemplify their unassimilable orientation to the Western world and potential harm if they come closer.[94] While it might be permissible for someone to eat an object that falls outside of normative expectations, it is not acceptable that one actively seeks out and desires such foodstuffs. Messages about what communities consume are a key part of maintaining rhetorical disidentifications as a visceral, gut-level response of disgust-based suspicion that orients the dominant demographics toward minorities at a necessary remove. The instinctual nature of this distance prevents recognition of broader systemic injustice and/or coalitional opportunities that might unmoor such hierarchical layers.

More broadly, the strategic connecting of Asianness and rats clarifies how racial hierarches are forged through assumptions and extrapolations about bodily desires that are primarily visible through an already racialized understanding of the connection between morality, eating, and embodiment. In future eras, the Chinese body would be seen as less of a direct threat to European American livelihoods, in part because beliefs on diet and physicality transformed outlooks from jealousy to pity. In 1928, USDA publicist T. Swann Harding argued that the lack of milk in Asian diets led to the Chinese being "peaceful, sequacious, unprogressive, unenterprising, non-persevering; his stature is poor, his physique bad, his mortality high."[95] The focus on milk, just like the prior obsession with meat, was wielded in service of racial hierarchies that "justified imperial projects of colonization."[96] The seeds for understanding Asian Americans as part of a unified and meek "model minority," in need of being subsumed within American ways of life, are clearly being laid here. Yet the belief that Asians must always fight deviant appetites that are different

93. I. Day, *Alien Capital*, 23.
94. Cannato, "How America Became Italian."
95. Harding, "Diet and Disease," 153.
96. DuPuis, *Dangerous Digestion*, 89.

than Western ones endures. As we will see in the next chapter, the fears that emerged during the coronavirus pandemic that began in 2020 are inseparable from a belief that Asian tastebuds are not merely dirty but deviant, spreading racial contamination as easily as flecks of spit spread COVID-19. The fear-based structures that enabled the metonymic linkages between rats and Asian bodies easily transfer to contemporary discussions about bats, coronavirus, and Asian contagion, once again rhetorically aimed at expelling an "Oriental" threat from US land.

CHAPTER 3

Bat Lovers

The Threat of Asian Appetites to
US National Embodiment

My parents barely ate meat   until the 1980s
In reeducation camps,   they ate ground pork
once a year   In America, we don't buy   live chickens,
but my mother always   wanted to see the fish
alive, head on before we take it   home.

—Sally Wen Mao, "Wet Market"

The year 2020 was marked by a global pandemic, raging wildfires, and political unrest. It was also marked by a notable uptick in violence against Asian Americans because of fear and misinformation about illicit wildlife vendors at Chinese wet markets as the probable origin of the coronavirus. The debate over the racial and geographic origin of a nonliving object demonstrates how the specter of the contaminated Asian is still available as a rhetorical prop for recentering racial hierarchies in the face of shifting global power dynamics. In order for whiteness to remain the unquestioned norm during a global pandemic where many Western leaders enacted ineffective or even harmful rhetoric and policies, the Asian must remain a stable signifier of foreign contagion.

The explicit shifting of attention to the virus's geographical origins amplified understandings of Asian consumption as an explicit threat to the nation through focusing on the deviant behavior of an abstracted individual Asian eater.[1] In a now deleted tweet, Michael Caputo, the then spokesman for the Department of Health and Human Services, claimed that "millions of Chinese suck the blood out of rabid bats as an appetizer and eat the ass out of anteaters" (March 12, 2020). This tweet crudely encapsulates "the heterosexual tribe's fear" of queerness, the fear of "being different, being other, and therefore lesser, therefore sub-human, in-human, non-human" as it manifests in rela-

---

1. Johnstone, "Rhetoric as a Wedge."

tion to eating.[2] Specifically, Caputo's remark captures how the assumed "alignment between oral pleasure and other forms of nonnormative desire" was and is rhetorically leveraged in order to render Asian bodies as a clear source of contagious deviance that threatens the stability of the US.[3] The hyperbolic escalation into the performance of sexual acts on vermalingua encapsulates how the orientation toward Asian bodies as always foreign is underpinned by a tacit belief that these forms of consumption are substantively different from Western ones and also masks for strange oralities underneath.

In this chapter, I argue that the furor over the coronavirus, blame of Asians as bat eaters, and associated anti-Asian violence are directly connected to the history of rhetorically positioning all Asian bodies as the wrong sort of eaters, forever beyond the realm of national belonging by virtue of their strange appetites. While the original discourse about the place of the "Chinaman" in the US emerged from specific fears about labor and masculinity in the late nineteenth century, the contemporary debates over the "China flu" and its link to Asian bodies echo those original accusations of deviance but manifest in a focus on queer orality. Defining Asian embodiment through its supposed predilection toward deviant sexuality dovetails with the ready assumption that perpetually foreign ontologies reveal themselves when eating; the yellow mouths that are assumed to always bear accents are also assumed to always yearn for something strange between the lips. Disgust with certain foods and sexual practices becomes a layered, satirical pastiche of a body that interchanges behaviors of sex and eating chaotically. The resulting gut orientation is one that defines Asian ontologies as all-consuming mouths that spread contagion through both alluring and repulsive practices, whether sexual or otherwise. Discussions of the purported links between Asian eating and COVID pivot on fears of what Mel Chen calls "queer licking," a "frightening originary scene of intoxication" that warns against the types of oral practices found in Asiatic realms.[4] In the era of a pandemic, this presumed strangeness of orifice acts as a connective glue, fusing a range of negative definitions of race, embodiment, and sexuality into a fictive, yet persuasive, ravenous Asian body that eats and fucks wrongly.

To demonstrate how the fears of Asian eating manifested in relation to broader discourses of national identification during the initial onset of COVID, I analyze artifacts that narrativize contagion through oppositional gut orientations toward Asian bodies. The rhetorical throughlines center Asian consumption and sexuality as both alluring because of their inherent

2. Anzaldúa, *Borderlands*, 18.
3. Tompkins, *Racial Indigestion*, 5.
4. M. Chen, *Animacies*, 185.

queer subordination and a threat to the embodied masculinity of the Western individual and nation. David Eng insists that "sexual and racial difference cannot be understood in isolation," specifically that "racial fantasies facilitate our investments in sexual fantasies and vice versa."[5] More specifically, the news stories and viral videos that affixed various levels of blame to Chinese bat eaters for the coronavirus pandemic rely on long-standing assumptions of Asian sexuality as a warped femininity; the Asian body is laden with disease from its strange forms of consumption, and it invites penetration in order to contaminate the masculine Western penetrator. Such fears about the threat of queer orality to individual bodies are nested within broader fears of threats to the nation's white, heteronormative, imperial power. In her study of post-9/11 depictions of terrorism, Jasbir Puar explores how terrorist bodies are labeled as not just racially other but also sexually deviant. These constructions perform "labor in the service of disciplining and normalizing subjects *away from* these bodies."[6] The audience is repulsed by the excessively queer eater even as it is satisfied by this confirmation of the rightness of non-Asian forms of consumption.

In this framework where the same desires that lead Asian eaters to alternatively consume or infect the vulnerable lead them to savagely devour helpless and rare animals, enacting physical violence against these bodies is transmuted into a necessary part of guarding the nation-state. In considering these depictions of Asian eaters, the fears about both the health of the nation and the individual body are distilled into fantasies of disgust with an isolatable figure—the bat eater—that can be excised from dinner tables and national belonging even as it motivates a queer sexual imaginary. Disgust's rhetorical force is paradoxical in how it "causes us to dwell on the material and sensory aspects of the object that disgusts us," which is "what lends disgust its peculiar magnetism even as it is an aversive reflex."[7] The fixation on the queerness of the Asian eater within the US is key to maintaining a hostile tolerance where *distance from* Asia on both a personal and national level is what prevents falling victim to this feminized perversity.

QUEER THREATS TO NATIONAL HEALTH

Asian identity within US borders has always been fraught. From the accusations of rat eating and "swarming" in the 1800s to the "yellow peril" of the

---

5. Eng, *Racial Castration,* 2.

6. Puar, *Terrorist Assemblages,* 38.

7. Khanna, *Visceral Logics,* 92.

1920s to the "model minority" of the latter half of the twentieth century, Asians are always something other than just American. As David Cisneros points out, the rhetorical function of borders is to "not only demarcate and divide but regulate relationships of contact, exchange, and equivalence between communities."[8] Racial stereotypes of identification work as borders between individuals on behalf of larger communities. In addition to geographical boundaries, the rhetorical bordering of the Asian body as always out of place within the space of the US performs a more subtle form of exclusion where the allowable range of contact and exchange is circumscribed by the ever-present suspicion of Asian flesh. While I will discuss how the over-homogenizing idealization of the model minority trope operates in chapter 5, I focus this chapter on the rhetorical messages surrounding Asian food and sex as revealing of "perpetually foreign" physiologies. These narratives of queer eating are inextricable from historical fantasies (and colonized socioeconomic constraints) of deviant Asian bodies whose primary function is to serve/service the white male soldier, and thus projects of Western expansion. Contemporary linkages of Asian eating, bats, and the coronavirus reaffirm Asian bodies as queer commodities rather than full citizens.

The link between Asians and disease has been leveraged at many points in history to overtly promote expulsion from the country and/or cordon populations off in Chinatowns and other segregated communities. The 1800s rhetoric around the eating of rats was used to denigrate Chinese embodiment as not-fully-human and as always shadowed with disease. Nayan Shah describes how the public health ills of San Francisco, including sewer systems ill-equipped to serve the rapidly growing city, were rhetorically framed as the contaminating influence of Chinatown rather than structural failures.[9] An illustration in *The Wasp* titled "San Francisco's Three Graces" enacts this epideictic blame, depicting the specters of Malaria, Smallpox, and Leprosy rising from Chinatown only to threaten all of San Francisco. The underlying fear of Asiatic contamination then and now enables predictions of future loyalties based on ties of culture and geography that are presented as evidence for the truth of the other. In these heuristics, it becomes possible to read a body's loyalty through both explicitly and implicitly marked characteristics of race.

In addition to serving more general logics of inclusion/exclusion, rhetorics that assume this determinism of birthplace rely on tacit beliefs in queer-er tendencies from faraway geographies. For example, those in the birther movement who claimed President Barack Obama was not a "natural-born citizen" and thus was ineligible to be president of the United States drew on rhetorical

---

8. Cisneros, *Border Crossed Us*, 6.
9. Shah, *Contagious Divides*.

FIGURE 3. "San Francisco's Three Graces," by George Frederick Keller.

structures that "re-inscribe perceived 'foreignness' as a racially coded boundary of acceptable citizenship."[10] Obama's signification of nonwhite racial heritage was coded not as a symbol of the American "melting pot" but as a sign
he was a "promiscuous global citizen" who threatened the US with outsider
doctrines.[11] The classificatory logic that reifies the idea that racial identity is

---

10. V. Pham, "Our Foreign President," 88.
11. V. Pham, "Our Foreign President," 90.

coterminous with geography and national boundaries also affirms certain races as more rightly deserving of US citizenship because they are assumed to be inherently inclined toward honesty and patriotism.[12] Such a belief in one's birthplace as manifest in one's being requires one ignore global trade and travel, and it erases the material realities of racial difference within a geographic location, marginalized subcultures, and those of mixed racial and/or ethnic heritage. Nonetheless, this reduction in nuance is easier to rhetorically leverage, especially to deny another's legitimacy as a sociopolitical actor.

For Asians in particular, non-US loyalty is always assumed to be an intrinsic aspect of the fundamentally strange and threatening yellow flesh. The "perpetual outsider" category is easily conflated with a general state of racial queerness, where to be not just nonwhite but "Oriental" is to be perpetually just beyond the reach of both cultural and ideological normativity.[13] Asians "who have achieved positions of authority or leadership routinely confront accusations that their foreignness makes them unfit for their jobs" due to invisible treacherous tendencies.[14] Even decorated war hero Daniel Inouye received "go back to Japan" attacks during his tenure as senator of Hawai'i. And throughout the spread of the virus and search for its origins, coronavirus and Communism were explicitly linked amidst discussions over whether the Chinese Communist Party's secrecy was a key factor in the rapid spread of the disease as well as the potential origin of the virus in a government lab. Within these scripts, everything that is Asian is also "born" in China, and thus must be a vector of both disease and Communism, infection and ideological wrongness.[15]

In the case of the coronavirus, the World Health Organization attempted to preemptively head off racial divides; the name for the virus, COVID-19, was "deliberately chosen to avoid stigmatization" based on race or nationality.[16] Despite these efforts, several prominent politicians and entertainment figures chose to use terms that directly connected the threat of coronavirus to China

---

12. Although most of the controversy focused on whether or not Obama was actually born in Kenya rather than Hawaii, it is worth noting that one strand of the birther movement claimed that Obama had switched both religions and citizenship when living in Indonesia as a child, associating him with Asian forms of religious and cultural strangeness.

13. I am adopted from Korea, and my sister is adopted from Vietnam. In both of our cases, multiple people explicitly asked our parents if we came from the southern parts of our countries, not the northern, Communist parts. We both were adopted at under six months of age.

14. Kim, "Racial Triangulation," 127.

15. During the bubonic plague outbreaks in San Francisco in the late nineteenth and early twentieth centuries, this same association of race, geography, and consumption was used against Asians. Dr. Walter Wyman wrote in 1900 that the bubonic plague was an "Oriental disease, peculiar to rice eaters" (qtd. in Shah, *Contagious Divides*, 155).

16. World Health Organization (@WHO), "DO—talk about the new #coronavirus disease . . ."

and Asian eating. There was a 650 percent increase of the term "Chinese virus" in retweets on Twitter by the end of March 8, 2020, and there was an 800 percent increase in the use of the term in news media by the next day.[17] The term "Wuhan virus" quickly spread on both traditional and social media, used by Mike Pompeo on *Fox and Friends* and Paul Gosar in tweets.[18] On March 19, Senator John Cornyn claimed that "China is to blame" because in "the culture where people eat bats and snakes and dogs and things like that, these viruses are transmitted from the animal to the people, and that's why China has been the source of a lot of these viruses like SARS, like MERS, the Swine Flu."[19] Bill Maher put it even more bluntly, proclaiming, "It's not racist to point out that eating bats is bat**** crazy," on his show *Real Time with Bill Maher*.[20]

Throughout 2020, President Donald Trump also used rhetoric that equated China, Asian embodiments, and disease. On March 10, he retweeted a tweet that used the term "China Virus" and then used the term himself on March 16. On March 19, 2020, a picture of the script for Trump's speech showed that the word "corona" had been crossed out and replaced with "Chinese," written in what appears to be his distinctive blocky handwriting. In response to repeated questions about why he insists on using the terms "Chinese virus" and "Wuhan flu" to refer to COVID 19, Trump stated that such phrases are not racist because "it comes from China, that's why." Although these efforts might have been aimed at providing a scapegoat for the haphazard governmental response to the virus in the US, these comments, echoed by many commentators online and in other media, recenter an enthymematic line of reasoning in which if something originates in a place, referring to it in racial terms is not racist but merely accurate. The rhetorical effect, however, is a welding of all people who live in such locales with the listed negative characteristics; race, nationality, and embodiment are naturally simpatico, and therefore disease of the body automatically scales upward to an ideologically warped nation state, and vice versa. This linkage generalizes a range of Asian bodies as phylogenetically predisposed to disorders of both the body and ethics, and it inscribes such beliefs into everyday discourse as easily accessible tropes. As Monica Chiu points out, "the color yellow in the term Yellow Peril conjures up images of disease (the yellow of jaundice, the sallow tone of unhealthy skin) and

---

17. Darling-Hammond et al., "After 'The China Virus,'" 870.

18. Darling-Hammond et al., "After 'The China Virus,'" 871.

19. The Hill, "Sen. John Cornyn." Such discriminatory language was not solely found in America; the French newspaper Le Courier Picard had run a front-page story with the headline "Coronavirus Chinois: Alert Jeune?" or "The Chinese Coronavirus: Yellow Peril?" in January 2020. In Australia, the Herald Sun ran a subtitle "*Chinese virus pandamonium*," punning on the presence of pandas in China, on an article about the virus (January 29, 2020).

20. *Real Time with Bill Maher,* April 10, 2020.

putrefaction (the unsightly hues of abscesses, blemishes, and infections)."[21] A feature of Asian physiognomy has been rhetorically reframed as scientific evidence of one's inherent physical contagion and the ongoing potential to irrupt into the body politic.[22]

Such rhetoric inscribes national borders on the level of the body, and the indexed affect influences what pathways of dealing with such bodies have the most incentives. Here, marking the Asian body as a vector of disease earned through eating is to mark it as an "abject" that *should* automatically evoke violent, bodily reactions in the non-Asian body.[23] To feel nausea when confronted with the specter of someone eating a bat is to affirm one's superior ethical position on a gut level. The non-Asian cannot help but be overcome by the appropriate affective sensations that compel them away from proximity to Asian bodies. It is not even necessary for there to be Asians in the immediate vicinity. Rather, what is important is the production of feelings that yield anticipation of such meetings as already suspect. The following examples from popular media demonstrate how the descriptions of the real, material threat of the coronavirus, even when more seemingly neutral, nonetheless perpetuate ideas about Asian embodiment as always requiring prophylaxis because of the queerness at its core.

WHERE ASIAN APPETITES ARE BRED

Consumption, as a tacit invitation into the body, is both an intimate arena to be policed and a performance of one's allegiance to national values and boundaries. Asian mouths are embedded within broader food systems that are inherently contaminated, and they cannot be trusted to filter out that which is poisonous, instead portrayed as permanently open and eager maws. The dominant portrayals of Asian foodways, particularly the now infamous wet markets, forward narratives of dirty spaces of purchase and consumption as the norm in Asian countries. COVID-19 is a zoonotic virus, a virus originat-

---

21. Chiu, *Filthy Fictions*, 6.

22. In a *New York Times* article titled "Eating Thai Fruit Demands Serious Effort but Delivers Sublime Reward," author Hannah Beach described the rambutan fruit as having "more than a passing resemblance to the coronavirus" (June 22, 2020). The article was criticized by many on social media for this and other comments that reproduced tropes of Asian food as "exotic" and potentially harmful. Food writer Osayi Endolyn performed a rhetorical analysis of the article on her Instagram account, pointing out how speaking of Asian fruit in terms of treachery and possible harm is part of a broader tendency toward "colonial rhetoric and framing" of Asian ways of life (June 24, 2020).

23. Yam, *Inconvenient Strangers*.

ing in animals and then passing to humans, and certain animals, bats and pangolins, were cited early on as potential vectors for the virus. In Western discussions of open-air markets, commonly referred to as wet markets, these places of commerce transform into queer liminal spaces where animals and humans mingle in strange ways that hint at slightly more camouflaged lascivities. Even prior to the outbreak of COVID, Asian foodways were popularly described in Western media as premodern in terms of civilization and food practices. On the popular reality TV show *Bizarre Foods* that aired in the early 2000s, host Andrew Zimmern described open-air markets in Tokyo and the Philippines, respectively, as evidence of how "Asians are very close to their food source" and "without any modern trappings."[24] These overgeneralizations not only elevate the Western audience member as part of a more civilized food ecology but also assume Asian eating as more queerly intimate—"very close"—with food objects.

The actual status of wet markets, like many cultural touchstones, varies by region and history. The etymology is apocryphal, but many say that the label of "wet" is related to the washing of produce and fish with hoses, leading to wet floors. An unbiased definition of wet markets understands them as a collectivity of private vendors in a public space where fresh food, such as fish and meat, is sold, often without extensive butchery or other processing. Under this definition, many permanent farmers markets in the US, such as the famed Pike Place Market in Seattle, would technically be wet markets. In many areas of China, these markets are such a part of the cultural fabric that they are still the main source of fresh vegetables for households despite the rise of Western-style supermarkets.[25] Importantly, the cultural role of this space is not homogenous, as there are ongoing issues across the country with how wildlife markets are managed that overlap with poaching and black-market trade. The demand and supply for the selling of wild animals, such as the pangolins that are now assumed to have been the primary vector for coronavirus, is part of a complex process of modernizing millennia-long traditions butting up against resistance to the encroachment of Western values on local customs.[26] Yet the nuance and contradictions of Asian wet market culture were not present in Western news coverage.

Instead, the headlines underscore wet markets as festering pits of contagion where all Asians go to gleefully buy and ingest animals with various degrees of naïveté or sordid aims. As "practices that systematically form the objects of which they speak," these media examples represent wet markets

---

24. Kelly, *Food Television*, 32.
25. Zhang and Pan, "The Transformation," 508–9.
26. Zhu and Zhu, "Understanding," 4.

as universally premodern locations, far removed from any consideration of hygiene or animal rights.[27] Although the topics of these articles are the potential animal source of contagion, the framing presents deviant, not-quite-human appetites as the underpinning of these markets' existence and filth. The *Wall Street Journal* published an article titled "Abolish Asia's Wet Markets, Where Pandemics Breed."[28] The *New York Times* ran "Where Bats Are Still on the Menu, if No Longer the Best Seller" with images of snakes and rats being sold at markets in Indonesia.[29] A *USA Today* article, "'A Loaded Gun': Wet Markets, Wildlife Trafficking Pose Threat for the Next Pandemic," assuredly states that wet markets are "where snakes, civets, and other exotic animals are sold along with more traditional livestock.[30] These, and many other headlines and articles, present snakes being sold alongside beef roasts as a daily practice and thus normalize Asian eating as based on consumption of beasts deemed unclean in Western cultures. In this framing, there is no room for discussion of regional variety, holiday-specific dishes, or how markets that sell exotic animals are perceived within various Asian contexts. The presentation of extreme behavior as the norm solidifies fears of the Asian outsider as observably factual.

These descriptions of overseas practices are interconnected with understandings of Asian eating as an insidious threat to domestic locales. In the United States, the idea that *all* Asians regularly eat dog often emerges in relation to concerns over the presence of new Asian immigrant populations in previously white neighborhoods. Robert Ji-Song Ku notes that a "typical urban legend features a mystery of someone's missing pug and the suspicious behavior of an immigrant family—typically Korean or Vietnamese—that recently moved to the neighborhood."[31] The rhetorical force of terms like "dog-eater" is grounded in the identificatory assumptions of not only the foreign nature of these bodies and their eating practices but also an inscrutable ethics that would render such practices palatable. The labeling, slurring, warns how the Asian tendency for eating such things is always threatening to emerge even within the civilizing context of Western culture. In a society where this trope is within easy reach, to be Asian is to risk having one's individual taste always framed as a matter of an entire geographical region's deviant orality. Frank Wu discusses how questions about myths of deviant eating, regardless of the

27. Foucault, *Archaeology*, 49.
28. Walzer and Kang, "Abolish Asia's 'Wet Markets.'"
29. Paddock and Sijabat, "Where Bats Are Still."
30. Shesgreen, "'A Loaded Gun.'"
31. Ku, *Dubious Gastronomy*, 54.

asker's intention, rhetorically project a more physically distant relationship between the asker and the askee.

> To the mocking inquiry, "Do Asians eat dogs?" no riposte, however sharp, can effectively convey that "I speak for myself alone." The question is common enough to list with the others that define the sensation of being a perpetual foreigner, so familiar to Asian-Americans, however well they can pass themselves off on the phone as White, and even if they are startled to see in the mirror that they are not: "Where are you *really* from?" and "How do you like it in our country?" and "When are you going home?"[32]

This fear of the consumption of domesticated animals is part of a broader racialized fear of unchecked animalism where the sensual experience of petting one's dog can become confused with eating it. The conversations about bats as food sources bear this same sense of misused senses, of devouring in a space that should only contain gentle, distanced contact. Whether the figure of the rat in the 1800s or bats in the twenty-first century, the actual animal under discussion does not really matter as long as it violates expectations for cleanliness and domestication and is thus able to signify the hypersensual overreach of warped consumption.

Even in a *Time* magazine article that actively attempts to *defuse* racist alarm about Asians as strange eaters, eating bats is still framed as a natural way of being for these unnatural bodies. The article opens with a third-person description of Li Rusheng, a local Yunnan province resident, and his hunting trips for bats from his youth. The first sentence is an anticipatory negation: "It wasn't greed, or curiosity, that made Li Rusheng grab his shotgun and enter Shitou cave. It was about survival."[33] The article then describes the level of poverty that meant Li and his fellow villagers would only eat meat once a year if not for the bats. Li's reflections on the practice of bat hunting and eating are quoted and framed in the following way.

> Li would creep into the gloom and fire blindly at the vaulted ceiling, picking up any quarry that fell to the ground, while his companions held nets over the mouth of the cave to snare fleeing bats. They cooked them in the traditional manner of Yunnan's ethnic Yi people: boiled to remove hair and skin, gutted and fried. "They'd be small ones, fat ones," says Li, now 81, sitting on a wall overlooking fields of tobacco seedlings. "The meat is very tender. But

32. Wu, *Yellow*, 41.
33. Campbell and Park, "Inside the Global Quest."

I've not been in that cave for over 30 years now," he adds, shaking his head wistfully. "They were very hard times."[34]

At first glance, this description seems relatively genuine in its attention to the intersection of economic hardship and cultural practices. There are no overt displays of writerly disgust. However, Li is positioned as a queerly consuming figure who does not align with the "cis-centric, sexually dimorphic, ableist conceptions of somatic normalcy."[35] The same vocabulary often used to describe bats and rodents is used to describe Li's hunting, a matter of "creeping" and firing "blindly," which evokes a sense of his body as both disabled and somehow naturally attuned to bat behavior, as an animal predator is to its prey. He is a feminized individual whose hunting success is a matter of luck rather than masculine skill. The sense of pleasure the Yi found in eating the bats, the "tender" meat, is coupled with the fact that they cooked them enough to have a "traditional" eating method. For example, Li describes the meat of the bats in ways akin to other livestock, grouped by size and in terms of the texture of its flesh, indicating a high level of intimacy with the animal. Although he is portrayed sympathetically, it is the presence of this sympathy that reinforces the idea that Asian tastes are beholden to a different sensory apparatus than that of Westerners. Asianness and queer desires of the mouth always coexist.

In more overtly negative linking of Asian bodies and the bestial, Asian appetite for these queer foods is centered as both a matter of cultural and individual desire. An online article that ran in various Australian newspapers with the tagline "It's enough to make your stomach turn" describes the Asian relationship to bats as follows:

> Unfortunately, the bat's exalted status as a traditional folk remedy means gourmands might not stop eating the flying rodents anytime soon. In Indonesia, a popular asthma cure involves removing a flying fox's heart like the evil priest in *Indiana Jones and the Temple of Doom* before cooking it and eating it, reports CNN. Even bat faeces is purported to cure everything from bad vision to childhood malnutrition in Chinese medicinal circles, reports the Yin Yang House.[36]

In this depiction, discussing Asian folk health traditions as a matter of consuming animal products reinforces the ideas that Asian bodies are less

---

34. Campbell and Park, "Inside the Global Quest."
35. Malatino, *Queer Embodiment*, 2.
36. "Horror Video."

healthy/more diseased than those of the presumed Western readers and that Asian forms of medical knowledge are hopelessly primitive in comparison. The possibility of alternative epistemological frameworks that involve different forms of contact with nature and animals is not mentioned. Instead, the use of bat parts for medicine is sarcastically framed as a matter of a peculiarly Asian orientation toward taste that is equal with the moral depravity of the "evil priest" in the Indiana Jones movie.

The rapid uptake of Asian embodiment as a natural source of COVID-19 led to statistically notable effects on the lives and livelihoods of Asian Americans. Along with the increase of verbal aggression, there was a worldwide rise in reported acts of violence against those of Asian descent following the use of these terms and linking of the virus to China. The Asian Pacific Policy and Planning Council (A3PCON), Chinese for Affirmative Action (CAA), and San Francisco State University's Asian American Studies Department started a website where people could report these actions on March 19, 2020. By September 2021, 10,370 incidents had been reported. In a press release from May 13, 2020, several of these incidents were anonymously quoted.[37]

- A couple walked by our street with a white dog in tow and the male took out a marker and tagged my parents' car with the word COVID 19 on the driver side door.
- was walking my dog at night and a car swerved toward me on the sidewalk, two guys started shouting, "Trump 2020, Die Chink Die!"
- was standing in an aisle at [a big box store] when suddenly I was struck from behind. Video surveillance verified the incident in which a white male using his bent elbow struck my upper back. Subsequent verbal attacks occurred with "Shut up, you Monkey!" "F**k you, Chinaman." "Go back to China" and ". . . bringing that Chinese virus over."

These incidents of hatred might be expected, but many of the accounts of violence and discrimination specifically reflect fears of deviant forms of eating. In September 2020, the Stop AAPI Hate Youth Campaign conducted a research study where they interviewed young adults across the US for how they had experienced the rising anti-Asian sentiment that accompanied the coronavirus pandemic. One in six of the youth reported having experienced verbal harassment or shunning in some form due to coronavirus-related fear, and 25.81 percent of the verbal harassment cases and 47.54 percent of online incidents directly referenced the assumed Chinese eating habits and/or the

---

37. "Stop AAPI Hate."

consumption of bats or dogs. A fifteen-year-old reported that his "classmate said that the pandemic is due to bad decision-making by Chinese people (referring to their eating bats) and aimed this comment at me because I was the only Asian student in that table."[38] An Asian teen recalled an incident at the airport in February 2020 when "a group of teenagers surrounded us and said, 'It smells like dog in here,' 'It smells like dang Coronavirus,' 'these eff-ing Asians,' and other derogatory terms."[39] These brief comments demonstrate how the assumptions of Asianness as a signal of foreign invasion are part of the same belief system that poses Asian forms of eating as a doorway to both disease and immoral forms of behavior. The performance of violent actions by non-Asians, centering the sensory offense of the presumed diet of bats with references to odor, is both a reaction to and proclamation of the correct forms of embodiment that are appropriately repulsed by gustatory deviance. Asian embodiment becomes evidence for forms of eating that do not have to be visible to be persuasive.

THE THREAT OF ASIAN ORIFICES

The fixation on bat eating as a danger to Western immune systems emerges from the same assumptions commonly found in narratives of the Asian female as a known sexual threat to the bodily integrity of Western men. Fears of both foodborne disease and STDs assume that the exotic allurement of Asianness tricks and then leads to direct harm for the non-Asian consumer. Much of the original anti-Chinese legislation in the late 1800s, including both local ordinances and national legislation like the Page Act of 1875, was purport-edly aimed at preventing the immigration of Asian prostitutes to the US to stop the spread of both immoral actions and venereal disease. This fear of harm from a treacherous Asian sexual partner permeates fictional and auto-biographical accounts alike. Will Eisner's graphic novel reporting on the Viet-nam War includes a short story titled "The Casualty," in which a soldier sleeps with a Vietnamese woman, only to be seriously injured when she plants a land mine under his bed.[40] In the film *Full Metal Jacket*, the Vietnamese prosti-tute (played by actress Papillion Soo) who memorably said "Me love you long time" is immediately described as diseased by Matthew Modine's character, Private Joker: "You know half these gook-whores are serving officers in the Vietcong? The other half have got TB. Be sure you only fuck the ones that

38. "They Blamed Me," 14.
39. "They Blamed Me," 13.
40. Eisner, *Last Day in Vietnam*.

cough."[41] Shortly after he says this, a Vietnamese man rushes up and steals the GI's camera. Whether the moral hurt of theft or the physical threat of STDs, the Asian female is too often used as a harbinger of harm to Western bodies.

The casual violence of these portrayals aligns with a long history of "white sexual imperialism" that explicitly commodified Asian female bodies for the pleasure of Western soldiers within the context of queer, nonpromulgating relationships. Mark Padoongpatt describes how the colonial practice of getting a "rented wife" or "duration wife" in Thailand led to viewing Thai women as "consumable objects—a national resource that made the lives of US servicemen easier and more leisurely."[42] In his remembrances of serving in Vietnam and Thailand, Gregory DeLaurier recounts how the dominant attitude of American soldiers toward Asian sex workers was oriented toward preventing disease, although not to the point of refusing sexual services.

> "Watch out for those LBFMs, son," said the sergeant. LBFMs? We'd only been in Thailand a couple of days and were about to hit the town for the first time. "Little Brown Fucking Machines, buddy. You don't want your dick to fall off do you?" He threw me a pack of condoms. "These Thai honeys'll fuck your brains out but goddamn won't they give you the clap." Forewarned, we went to town.[43]

The "LBFMs" that DeLaurier refers to were most likely part of the "Rest and Recreation" facilities, known as "Intoxication and Intercourse" centers by soldiers, that were explicitly designed for the comfort of US military men via agreements between the US and Southeast Asian governments.[44] US soldiers in Southeast Asian during the 1970s knew that they could get "a girl for the price of a burger" who should be willing to yield all "three holes."[45] The "girl" is not just cheap but offering the use of orifices that do not fit with the dominant heteronormative narratives that accompany domestic white marriages. The level of actual willingness will vary from "girl" to "girl," but the overarching rhetorical framework for understanding Asian sexuality underscores the overflowing excess of sexual capacity. Yet the satisfaction of this encounter is also posited as equal to consuming fast food, a move that frames Asian sexuality as disposable, easily replaceable, and not very healthy. Specifically, purchased Asian sexuality is both novel and temporary, just queer enough. Such fram-

41. Kubrick, *Full Metal Jacket*.
42. Padoongpatt, *Flavors of Empire*, 36.
43. DeLaurier, "Thailand 1970," 232.
44. Woan, "White Sexual Imperialism," 284.
45. Woan, "White Sexual Imperialism," 283, 285.

ing walks a tight line between what Jasbir Puar describes as the separation between "upright, domesticable queernesses that mimic and recenter liberal subjecthood, and out-of-control, untetherable queerness."[46] In other words, these sexual encounters clearly take place outside of heteronormative marriages and progeny formation but are allowable as part of the project of nation building and expansion; the Asian body's deviant sexuality is temporarily controlled through its association with service to white male US soldiers.

In cases where Asian male sexuality is discussed, it is framed as a threat to the social order of American life via queer orality that results in miscegenation. For example, the rhetoric used to rail against opium dens during the 1800s centered fears about bodily proximities and intimacies as gateways to interracial bodily contact. The actual dens were often small, basement-level spaces where smokers would recline nearby to or in direct contact with other smokers. Even without direct bodily contact, the opium pipe stem became a focus point for those afraid of oral contact with the Asian Other. Nayan Shah argues that the "panic of ingesting the residues of bodily fluids and of sucking a pipe shared by multiple, anonymous mouths emphasized the promiscuous orality of the experience."[47] And this "promiscuous orality" was assumed to automatically lead to other forms of promiscuity, with Dr. Harry Hubbell Kane arguing that "many females are so much excited sexually by the smoking of opium during the first few weeks" that they are easily seduced by Chinese lovers.[48] However hyperbolic or fearmongering these descriptions are, the queer threat of miscegenation was seen as directly resulting from oral contact with this Asian substance.

The assumption of queer orality that abuts derangement permeates discourse around bat eating and the rise of the coronavirus. Early in 2020, several videos of food bloggers eating bats were put forth as evidence of both inherent Asian desires and the "smoking gun" of the start of coronavirus, rather than as the form of stunt eating regularly seen in extreme food television shows. One video, from 2016, shows the food blogger Wang Mengyun trying bat soup in Palau, not China, yet it was nonetheless cited in several news articles as causal of the development and spread of the coronavirus.[49] The other most viral video, uploaded to the YouTube channel Russia Today and embedded in

---

46. Puar, *Terrorist Assemblages,* 47.

47. Shah, *Contagious Divides,* 95.

48. Ahmad, "Opium Smoking," 59.

49. See Darrach, "The New Coronavirus" for an interview with Kent Ono about news coverage of COVID-19. Ono points out how the repeated references to bat guano are a throwback to the anti-rat/anti-Chinese rhetoric from the late 1800s. He states, "Figuratively, a bat is a flying rat. The implication is that if humans in China are touching *guano* (bat dung), it marks the entire culture as unsanitary."

FIGURE 4. Screenshot from "Video of Woman Eating
Whole Bat Emerges as Scientists Link Coronavirus to
the Flying Mammals," Twitter, January 25, 2020.

numerous links and news stories, was titled "Video of Woman Eating Whole
Bat Emerges as Scientists Link Coronavirus to the Flying Mammals."[50] In this
video, the woman (a different woman from Wang) is holding the bat over a
bowl of soup with chopsticks, and she gently nibbles at one of the bat's wings.
In this short clip, she never actually takes a bite out of the bat, finally looking
up at the end at her friends off camera who are speaking Chinese, coaching
her on where to bite. Despite not managing to eat any of the bat, the display
of Asian lips on a bat's wings was taken as concrete evidence of both her and
all Asian eaters' "promiscuous orality."[51]

The comments on this video reflect the prestanding belief that all Chinese
people hold the same form of indiscriminate taste and regularly practice these

50. During the Russian invasion of Ukraine in 2022, the Russia Today YouTube channel
was taken down. The same video was uploaded in many other places on the web and received
similar comments in those locations.

51. Shah, *Contagious Divides*, 95.

forms of strange consumption: "They eat anything and everything that is moving," "Rodents, insects, dogs, cats and babies, nothing is off limits," and "If it doesn't eat them first, the Chinese will eat it raw and call it a delicacy." This theme of "Chinese people will eat anything" and "anything that moves" trope, perhaps even to the point of cannibalizing helpless infants, works to position Chinese consumption as not only disgusting but also as a method of being in the world that automatically leads to the crossing of moral boundaries. The rhetorical use of cannibalism has long been used to signal "a certain imaginative and ethical limit" that marks "civilizational otherness."[52] Saying that a people "eat everything" could in itself just be a description of a broader digestive capacity, but the placing of rodents and babies side by side as potential edible objects clarifies how this breadth is actually meant to signal either an amoral lack of judgment or a more intentional instance of evil. Sara Ahmed points out how the "speech act, 'It's disgusting!' becomes 'They are disgusting,' which translates into, 'We are disgusted by them.'"[53] Here the figure of a bat as a source of contamination infuses not just the depicted eater but all bodies that can be read as Asian with uncleanliness. The they "who eat everything" become automatic sources of disgust to those who curate their plates more carefully.

Although eating something that is still alive is often practiced even in the West (oysters), such explicit relating of the rawness of flesh to explicit desire frames certain modes of eating as excessive and illegitimate. In writing about sushi and its popularity in a US context, Anne Anlin Cheng argues that the confrontational presentation of raw flesh "insists on its fundamental otherness [. . .] and it does so not through its apparent racial sign, or through its supposedly exotic origin, but instead through its disruptive effects on our 'human' ontology. In short, sushi eating *queers* its eater, not by being foreign per se, but paradoxically by being too intimate."[54] To eat raw meat is to invite a sensual intimacy via contact of different fleshes that is controlled through the acts of chewing and swallowing. The line between the flesh of the human tongue and the inside of a mackerel's flank is one of function, not of kind. Yet in the case of sushi, this intimacy is masked through the removal of all identifying aspects of the animal, such as eyes and fins. The remaining piece of flesh is both physically and imaginatively easier to swallow; one can deny any connection with the bestial even as one enjoys the pureness of flavor and texture that are destroyed in the more civilized act of cooking. In the food blogger videos, bat eating instead highlights the sensual experience of nipping with one's teeth

---

52. Roy, *Alimentary Tracts*, 13.
53. Ahmed, *Cultural Politics*, 98.
54. A. Cheng, *Ornamentalism*, 112.

at the smooth skin of an animal's back, trying to find the deanimated flesh underneath. This form of eating is repellent not only because of the object of the bat but for how it exposes tendencies of the mouth. If the Asian is willing to enter into queer oral practices when eating, then those same body parts must also be more prone to transgression in other areas as well.

I now turn to an animated clip from 2020 of an Asian female figure dancing with and then kissing a bat that responded to and went semi-viral during the initial furor over the origin of COVID. In this clip, an Asian female cartoon partakes in deviant oral relations, both eating and kissing pangolins and bats. The mockery of Asian eating through a mockery of Asian sex illustrates how easily these carnal acts slide together in the imaginings of Asianness.[55] As Leslie Bow states, "Ethnic caricature is not cute; indeed, it constitutes a form of hate speech."[56] Yet I focus not solely on the crude hatred embedded in this clip but rather on how the potency of the Asian female body is the simultaneous presence of the erotic and the grotesque. The video exemplifies how the already assumed queerness of Asian orality both manifests in fears of Asian eating and supports the continued fraught allure of encounters with the sexual Other.

Sven Stoffels is an animator who has worked with CollegeHumor and Comedy Central. He posted the video he made to his Twitter account on April 22, 2020, with the caption and hashtags "Corona CHingChan does a 'lil dance for us. #corona #covid19 #chinesevirus #chinavirus." The video quickly received widespread negative attention. YouTube eventually removed the video in response to complaints, although it was eventually reposted under another title. A petition for Patreon to remove Stoffels from their platform was started, but it failed to garner the targeted number of signatures. After some of the controversy had faded, Stoffels tweeted, "When will China take legal and financial responsibility for a health crisis and viral pandemic that ravaged nations worldwide? #cancelchina" on May 12, 2020.

Stoffels's uptake of blaming China for the coronavirus might have been more performative than revealing of inner beliefs. Regardless, the choice of racist tropes in his animation demonstrates the convergence of fears of the nonlimits of Asian female sexuality and contact with its queerly devouring body. Or, the humor of pairing these hyperbolic portrayals of sexual excess in direct juxtaposition with grotesque consumptions of vile animals is only successful if the audience shares a belief that Asian female embodiment is always

---

55. The television show *South Park* went even further in its satire of the coronavirus pandemic with an episode that had one of the main characters lusting after and then having sex with a bat.

56. Bow, "Racist Cute," 34.

already a little queer, always beyond the limits of the norm. Her violation of the line between animal and human is then not just an individual choice but representative of a virus-spreading wrong against both her sexual partners and the broader non-Asian world.

The choice to do a short animation allows Stoffels to perform these tropes of Asian femininity as hyperbolic overrepresentations and thus to claim misunderstood humor in response to accusations that he is perpetuating racial ideas. However, to accept this explanation would be to ignore how race is itself defined through scales of intensity. The racial Other is consistently depicted as an overly animated being who is regularly moved to exceed the bounds for emotional and physical expression. As Sianne Ngai argues, in American culture, "animation remains central to the production of the racially marked subject, *even* when his or her difference is signaled by the pathos of emotional suppression rather than excess."[57] Racially marked bodies are always *more*, and Asian women are always "simultaneously *more than* and *too much*."[58] The racially animated body is held to be synonymous with the agitated body, a body that is in need of suppression.[59] The choice of medium both amplifies the presumed queer, devouring orality through the visual hyperbole of animation and attempts to reassert control over the unruly Asian body that spouts excess in unacceptable ways.

The central female figure in Stoffel's animation is a bricolage of sexual and repulsive stereotypes set in opposition to one another. The video is organized as a series of bait and switches where the first shot oversexualizes a portion of the female figure's body, but then a quick reveal shows the grotesque underpinnings. The figure is clad in a bikini and has a slim figure that fits the standards for Asian beauty. Her hair is done up in pigtails that mimic the portrayal of ancient Chinese dress. The opening shot is of her bottom, wiggling side to side in a sexual dance to the background music full of vaguely Asian-sounding string and flute instruments. Yet even as the figure is clearly sexualized from the beginning, she is also adorned with the grotesque aspects of Asian stereotypes. After the opening shot, the female turns her head to smile at the viewer, squinting through "slitty" eyes and with a full mouth of splayed buckteeth. In another shot, she hides her face demurely behind a fan, reminiscent of depictions of geisha, a gesture that turns grotesque when she lowers the fan to reveal mucous dripping from her nose and teeth clamped around body parts of partially chewed insects and animals. Another scene shows her dancing while wearing a bra that resembles the coronavirus spiky orbs. She holds two

57. Ngai, *Ugly Feelings*, 95.
58. Raymundo, "Beauty Regimens," 113.
59. M. Chen, "Agitation."

FIGURE 5. Screenshot of skinned pangolin from "Corona
CHingChan does a 'lil dance for us," Sven Stoffels, April 22, 2020.

pangolins, one in each hand, the one in the left hand flayed and skinned to
reveal its rodent skull.

Again, the fear of the Asian figure centers on its supposed oral tendencies.
Kyla Wazana Tompkins sketches what she deems *"queer alimentarity,* a form
of nonnormative sensuality that centers on orality and the mouth."[60] This idea
"of eating as a form of sensual pleasure that works against the nation's interests," the belief that certain forms of eating are both deviantly excessive and
sexually gratifying, is clearly manifest in the hyperbolic nature of Stoffels's
animation.[61] And this figure is most assuredly queer. She is not bothered by
her excessive body but rather seems to revel in the unchecked sensuality that
involves physical contact with animals. In the scene where she reveals her
mouth full of insects and dripping nose, she nonetheless waggles her eye-
brows suggestively. She aggressively consumes these insects and other animals,
spreading her viral load through the saliva that drips out of her mouth as she

60. Tompkins, *Racial Indigestion,* 68.
61. Tompkins, *Racial Indigestion,* 69.

swallows. Stoffels's portrayal of the aberrant as coequal with the erotic maintains Asian embodiment as that which is to be approached cautiously and at
risk of being sensorially offended.[62]

Even as the animated female plays off of constructions of Asian women
as hypersexual, it violates other expectations of sexual appeal via a performance of bestiality that encapsulates broader xenophobic fears.[63] Notably, a
central portion of the clip focuses on the female figure aggressively kissing
a bat. The only movement during these few seconds is that of the woman's
tongue wiggling in an obscene parody of a passionate kiss inside of the bat's
gaping, toothed jaw. Such a creative choice reflects broader patterns of negotiating xenophobic fears through projection onto the threat of the animal. Ruptures in the social fabric, such as a global virus threat, are places where "many
axes of human difference collide [. . .] if the animal figure mediates many of
these axes, then it becomes a condensed and explosive discursive site."[64] It is
not just the portrayal of supposed desire for an animal that is so unseemly.
Rather, as the entire clip is explicitly contextualized in relation to the spread
of the coronavirus from China into other countries, the exaggerated enaction of human-animal desire expresses the fear of mixing of races and nations
as the first step toward queer relationships. The female figure is clearly not
operating within the bounds of a heteronormative marriage, and the linking
of her sexuality and animal consumption renders her reproductive capacity a
potential biopolitical threat to, in this case, global economies. Bats are already
vampiric figures of fear and horror in Western culture, but the visual depiction
of these interactions is deliberately queered further. Eating a dead bat, with
its teeth slightly bared, is rendered equal with the bestial desire to French kiss
it. Although not explicitly cast as an argument for who is responsible for the
spread of coronavirus, this portrayal of Asian female sexuality as hyperdeviant
consumption is presented as the logical limit case of Asiatic eating, pinning
the origin of the virus on Asian bodies that yearn for such transgressive habits.

The warping of the image of the docile Asian beauty into a being that
manages to be sexually alluring despite her bodily tendencies toward disease
amplifies the historicized assumption about Asian sexuality as inherently
"pathological spaces of violence that are constituted as sexually excessive,
irrational, and abnormal."[65] In the shot where the female figure holds two

62. In 2018 there was a spate of anti-Chinese graffiti in the neighborhood of Bensonhurst,
Brooklyn, that read "Chinese Cunts Stink Like Fish."
63. Celine Parreñas Shimizu points out that judgments of hyper- or excessive sexuality are
leveled from "white male sex as normative position" ("Bind of Representation," 252).
64. M. Chen, *Animacies*, 100.
65. Puar, *Terrorist Assemblages*, 71.

FIGURE 6. Screenshot of woman kissing a bat from "Corona CHingChan does a 'lil dance for us," Sven Stoffels, April 22, 2020.

pangolins, she dances in a sexually suggestive manner while wearing underwear, knee socks, and a bra drawn to resemble the coronavirus. The placement of coronavirus spheres over the breasts makes for a cheap visual pun, but it also speaks to the underlying fear of the "gook-whore" that marks the allure/deception image of the Asian sexual partner. Coronavirus is transmitted through saliva and mucus, through spitting and sneezing, or through sucking and swallowing. Covering the Asian female's mammary glands with images of the coronavirus offers a clear message as to the danger embedded within the Asian body. The two pangolins queer the image further, as the one in her left hand is in the process of being butchered, presumably for eating. If to consume this female body sexually is thus to consume the essence of the repulsive animal, the future sexual partner is warned about the potential queer contamination of their own body should they choose to suckle at this same teat.

The main concern when considering such a video is how the satirical presentation of racial fears, presented as "just a joke," reinforce and further disseminate understandings of Asian embodiment as on the precipice of deviance. The Asian woman is always understood as inherently more sexual than white woman, inhabiting a self that is so sensuous that it even risks tipping into a sloppy bestiality. Attending to how such portrayals incline the viewer's body away from the Asian female figure is especially important because of how "desire and disgust are dialectically conjoined."[66] The pairing of these two ideas inside a queer, ravenous mouth produces attitudes toward Asian embodiment as a space of potential titillation but also where full intimacy is dangerous.

CONCLUSIONS

These continued portrayals and performances of hyperanimated racial eaters are rhetorical instances that are inextricable from the parallel instances of violence that constrain real bodies. The contemporary narratives connecting bats, Chinese individuals, and the coronavirus draw on existing rhetorical structures that render Asian bodies, disease, and sexual taboos coequal. As we saw in chapter 2, the strategies used to render Chinese in a metonymic relationship with rats recur in contemporary stereotypes about eating dogs and, since 2020, bats and pangolins. The preference for eating these animals is premised on a tautological loop where an assumed degraded physiology with a taste for the debased is assumed to be evidence for other sexual proclivities, and vice versa. It is not just that the Asian body craves disgusting meals but that such appetites transfer both to the sexual acts they partake in and their potential sexual partners. The beliefs in nonnormative eating and sex are easier to swallow when reproduced in tandem.

The news stories about bats in China, videos of the blogger eating a bat, and Stoffels's cartoon are fragments of the broader discourses about Asianness, animality, and contamination circulating while acts of physical violence, some to the point of hate crimes, increase and spread. The range of these texts demonstrates the ease with which existing tacit beliefs about Asian eating, sexuality, and deviance fit into contemporary understandings of racial physiologies. For rhetoricians invested in studying embodiment, the case of the coronavirus is instructive as to the roughly tangled trajectories and relative power of cultural scripts and material bodies. Rhetorics of racial consumption in particular can foster rhetorical orientations that reinforce certain bodies as requiring careful handling and prevent engaging with the individual in their fullness.

Although the term and identity category of "queerness" have been productively reclaimed by many, the tangled set of assumptions about race and sex attached to certain bodies means that discriminatory definitions of queerness

---

66. Ngai, *Ugly Feelings*, 332–33.

are still very active and suasive. Particularly, to be an Asian female within such a geography is to exist in tension with the contradictory expectations of being hypersexual for others' consumptive pleasure yet passive enough to be the type of body others want to consume. An Asian female body that produces impacts beyond titillation or distant admiration is therefore both aesthetically and racially wrong, a double betrayal. Ersula Ore clarifies how collective violence, such as lynching, "is a rhetorical enterprise intended to forge and maintain alliances, create and sustain community, and direct future action."[67] The violent attacks on Asian women, where many of the assaulters yell some version of "Go back to where you came from," reinforce orientations toward Asian women as a barely tolerated threat to an American future. In April 2020, a Brooklyn woman was attacked by a man who threw acid on her face and neck when she took out her trash, such purposeful maiming a clear attack on the woman's appearance as well as her life. Several of the reports that involve Asian women, often alone, report sucker punches, spitting, or other physical attacks. In July 2020, two masked assailants slapped and then set an eighty-nine-year-old woman on fire. In March 2021, a shooter who claimed "sex addiction" as his reason for murdering massage workers killed, among others, six Asian women in Atlanta, Georgia. These, among numerous other acts of explicit violence, promote disidentification with Asianness, but more insidiously, they recirculate assumptions of Asian embodiment as always so diseased as to require a violent shove away.

In the next chapter, we see how the expectation of "easy consumption" of Asianness is enacted on people's plates. I take up strands of recent discourses in wellness and "clean eating" to show how such discourses elevate themselves via direct opposition to the hyperstimulation of Asian food. In considering the forms of embodiment these discourses promise, I argue that these food creators and influencers are not just reacting based on personal taste. Rather, they are enacting fears about the boundaries of the Western body through persuasive instances of *phantasia,* the imaginative description of the sensorial and the sensual, as a form of eating-based identification. In order to align with these dominant discourses, the eater must be in an alert, anticipatory state for any signs of "agitation" that are preventatively identified with states of unhealth.[68]

---

67. Ore, *Lynching,* 54.
68. M. Chen, "Agitation."

CHAPTER 4

MSG Users

Phantasies of Health as Race Neutral

In February 2021, protestors, activists, and politicians gathered and marched to #StopAsianHate in New York City. Alongside the signs calling for an end to violence and to support Asian American pride, one sign, and its various permutations, directly addressed the interconnection of anti-Asian racism and exploitation in terms of consumption—"Love Our People Like U Love Our Food."[1] The enthymemic pointedness of such a sign gets at a question that is surprisingly still at the heart of Asian and American race relations in the twenty-first century: Why, given the popularity of Asian food in Western culture, are the Asian bodies that potentially create this food still targeted for violence and harassment with such frequency? I argue that such cognitive dissonance is rooted in assumptions that the spice and stimulation of Asian food that produces pleasure when eating is assumed to reflect an inherent level of lowered wellness of Asian embodiment. The equation of Asian identity with tasty food and novel food practices is all too easily flipped from a positive to a negative in the rhetorical framing of Asian communities, evidenced both in the case of scapegoating Chinese male immigrants during the late 1800s (chapter 2) and in the twenty-first-century violence against Asians and Asian Americans during the COVID-19 pandemic (chapter 3). The ongoing negative rhetorical engagement with Asian food and food practices demonstrates how

---

1. Venugopal, "Demonstrators, Elected Officials."

eating a group's food might amplify tacit feelings of disdain and resentment due to direct encounters with feelings that fall beyond normative registers of sensation and are therefore reframed as *over*stimulation.

In this chapter, I shift away from looking at rhetorics that figure the Asian body as a deviant eater and toward how Asian food is seen as causal of Asian-type sensations and reflective of the flawed Asian embodiment that would cultivate such cuisine. The beliefs wielded in discourses around queerness and animal-adjacent filth related to rat or bat eating also manifest in more covert suspicion of Asian objects related to food and consumption. Trends in health and wellness discourse, particularly in relation to nutrition, posit the Asian plate as a one-dimensional, one-ethnicity hostile foil to Western well-being practices and products. Particularly, Asian food is placed in opposition to the lifestyle/diet approach of "clean eating," an opposition connected to long-standing stereotypes of the dirty immigrant kitchen. Yet this opposition is achieved not through overt blame of racial categories, ethnic traditions, or class markers but rather through the placing of vivid descriptions of previous ill experiences into cautionary forecasts for one's bodily future. Generally, the discourse surrounding food is full of richly imaginative rhetorics that draw on phantasia, the evoking of remembered visuals and sensations. Within the prominent subset of wellness culture, a culture that prioritizes physical sensation as a metric for gauging one's present and future physical health, the sensations caused by Asian food can quickly become shoehorned into a framework of "good" and "bad" foods from the supposedly neutral stance of a benevolent outsider. Because of the intimate, experiential nature of these sensations, critiquing the foods and practices that cause them perpetuates race- and class-based hierarchies without direct reference to race or class themselves. Rather, maintaining distance between the body of the eater and the presumed effects of Asian food preparation is rhetorically cast as a matter of self-protection or improvement. The logics of deviance associated with gender and sexuality, including contamination and ill-health, emerge even when the Asian body itself is not present through beliefs in appropriate forms of sensation and stimulation.

To make this case, I trace how the assumptions that rendered the pathologizing of monosodium glutamate (MSG) suasive in the 1960s and '70s and that reemerged in the discourse of wellness influencers in the 2010s are both grounded in suspicions of the sensory experience of eating ethnic food as a sign of inherent harmfulness. After briefly discussing how MSG was made to be and remains controversial in the public sphere, I turn to the case of restaurateur and wellness influencer Arielle Haspel. I analyze Haspel's discourse on her restaurant, Lucky Lee's, and on her health blog as a way of unpacking how definitions of "clean eating" posit "problems of health and their solutions principally, although not exclusively, as matters within the boundaries of personal control" while relying on raced and classed understandings of what sensations eating should evoke.[2] In Haspel's case, even as she opened her own restaurant that proffered "healthier" versions of Chinese food, she categorized all Chinese food as that which would make you feel "bloated and icky." The example of Haspel and Lucky Lee's demonstrates how suspicions of the Asian body are ever present in suspicions of Asian food as a threat to the non-Asian eater, overstimulating and rupturing the Western belly. MSG and other Asian substances are refigured as objects of *dis-taste*, where the bodily reaction to these is a signal of moral sensation.

As my analysis of these controversies around health, wellness, and Asian sources of nutrition will demonstrate, believing Asian food is a universal source of unhealthiness is convincing because of the belief that bodily reactions to racialized objects are individually formed rather than embedded within broader threads of racial bias that accrue on the level of taste. Many scholars have already noted how the commodification of Asian objects and practices in Western contexts, such as skincare and yoga, results in a decontextualized echo of the original that is aimed at serving the self-actualization of upper-class white women.[3] I extend this ongoing discussion of rhetorics of cultural appropriation by examining how the sensory becomes its own evidence for healthy embodiment through classist, racist assumptions that explain undiagnosable sensations as harbingers of future ill-health. From this space of a supposedly neutral focus on health, the idea of rejecting an unhealthy ethnic food in favor of a white-produced version becomes not about racism but about protecting the body. Crucially, the evidence for these sorts of arguments is not explicit discussion of the minority group in question but rather a discussion of the effect of said minority groups' products or practices on the individual, nonminority body. Such rhetorical positioning centers a body that feels in a cultivated way rather than one that directly attends to visual or discursive markers of race. It is this shift from the visible to the visceral, from visualizing phantasmagoria of rat and bat eaters to feeling phantasms within, that is key.[4]

---

2. Biltekoff, *Eating Right in America*, 90.

3. See LeMesurier, "Race as Supplement"; Shome, *Diana and Beyond*; and Vats, "(Dis) owning Bikram."

4. See Smith, *How Race Is Made*, for a discussion of where feeling has been used as a measure of an Other's race in the absence of overt markers, as with anti-miscegenation discourses that claimed one could smell Blackness in those who otherwise were able to pass as white.

Specifically, the rhetoric that centers uncomfortable bodily sensation as evidence of the harmful nature of Asian food is grounded in language designed to evoke phantasia, an evoking of remembered sensation as evidence for rhetorical judgment. Ancient Greek thought emphasizes phantasia as a visual matter, where what "is absent before the eyes physically is made present to the mind through *lexis,* in the same way that an individual may 'put' images before her mind while imagining."[5] Misti Yang rethinks this concept with the stoics as more of a "rhetorical impression" that "evokes events, movements, and feelings, and supports a rhetoric that takes physiological incitement seriously."[6] In short, phantasia's rhetorical power is in the drawing of resonances between vivid past experiences and the present moment, producing bricolages of affect, imagery, and sensation that influence both perception and interpretation. In many uses of phantasia, the reification of epideictic categories of praise and blame related to food/eating can easily incorporate existing biases about race and class into broader messages around health and the boundaries of the body. Wellness discourse, while trendy, does not exist in isolation from the socioeconomic biases that maintain certain types of ethnic cuisine as permanently excluded from higher-class and/or elite status.[7] The prominent use of phantastic bodily images to categorize food into binaries of good/bad, moral/immoral, creates rhetorical space to substitute versions of Asianness that more readily align to exogenously decided upon standards for eating and sensation that remain within white, middle-class norms. As part of the overarching system of racial capitalism that equates wealth with whiteness, the yoking together of foods and sensations also maintains the apparent objectivity of high-end versus low-end foods within the space of the body itself. Eating, as an arena that lends itself to imaginative phantasia, can easily be underwritten by toxic orientations.

"TURNED ON" BODIES

Drawing on sensory experiences and heightened bodily feelings is a key part of fostering public action in opposition to objects perceived as threatening. Energetic, kinetic language evokes physical sensations and spatial terrains, fostering pathways for available rhetorical action. Jenell Johnson details how the controversy over fluoridation relies on the rhetorical creation of "visceral

---

5. O'Gorman, "Aristotle's *Phantasia,*" 24.
6. M. Yang, "Phantastic, Impressive Rhetoric," 389.
7. Ray, *Ethnic Restaurateur.*

publics" that "cohere by means of intense feeling."[8] The visceral "concerns the surfaces and orifices—the skin, the mouth, the lungs, the alimentary tract—that link the inside to the outside and the body-as-subject to the body-as-object, the porous membranes that bring the body and world into relation."[9] In other words, the intensity of emotion and affect that emerges in response to contact between the body and the world can quickly become evidence for understanding such contact as a natural limit. Similar to how rhetorical scholars have seriously grappled with the complex rhetorical strategies of anti-vaccination individuals that rely on bodily sensation and lived experience, it is worth investigating what the particular strategy of relying on remembered bodily experience, rather than scientific evidence, allows individuals to rhetorically preserve in discussions around race and food.[10]

The felt sense of viscerality is often motivated "in response to any border transgression that becomes an issue of public concern."[11] Modern examples of rhetorically framing Asian food as nutritionally suspect rely on sensory evidence that interlinked physical and moral boundaries are weakening. The prevalent myth that monosodium glutamate, or MSG, is harmful is grounded in tacitly racist ideas about Chinese cuisine and culture as full of strange, potentially harmful substances that cause immediate disturbance to the consuming body.[12] The initial health scare has faded somewhat, but the metonymical relationship between MSG and Chinese food still resonates, hence why Chinese restaurant owners the world over continue to have "No MSG" signs in their windows and on their tabletops. Although the Federal Drug Administration labels MSG as "generally recognized as safe," only causing reactions inconsistently in a very small number of people, there are still fears that MSG is a trigger of everything from headaches and nausea to the urge to take off all of your clothing.[13] The two separate assumptions that have become conflated—MSG is harmful to one's health in a number of sneaky, unpredictable ways, and MSG is inherently Chinese—rely upon the reproduction of phantasia related to eating at Chinese restaurants gone wrong.

The link between MSG and Chinese food was originally based on multiple testimonies about strange bodily agitation that violates the normative level and intensity of sensation. In his original letter to the *New England Journal of Medicine* querying if other doctors had noticed potential effects from "North-

8. Johnson, "'A Man's Mouth,'" 2.
9. Johnson, "'A Man's Mouth,'" 5.
10. Campeau, "Vaccine Barriers."
11. Johnson, "'A Man's Mouth,'" 14.
12. See LeMesurier, "Uptaking Race" and Mosby, "'That Won-Ton Soup Headache.'"
13. Kleiman, "Chinese Food Make You Crazy?"

ern Chinese" restaurants, Dr. Ho Man Kwok described "numbness at the back
of the neck, general weakness and palpitation" as the result of eating at such
places.[14] Kwok mentioned a range of possible reasons for these feelings, such
as cooking alcohol or high sodium content, and he limited his focus to a small
subset of Chinese restaurants. However, the news media seized upon the presence of MSG at all Chinese restaurants as a universal cause of these symptoms.
The "emotive visualization" of phantasia conflated fears of chemical contamination and xenophobia into a clearly defined cause-and-effect relationship
between eating Chinese food and symptoms as wide-ranging as eye pressure
and chest pain.[15] One of the researchers who originally conducted small-scale
studies on MSG, Dr. Herbert Schaumburg, described the sensory experience
of MSG as "it's almost like turning on. It's not really unpleasurable, once you
realize you're not going to die."[16] The linking of MSG to "turning on," a sensation clearly not within the realm of Western-style eating, brackets Chinese
food as firmly within the realm of the phantastic, sensorially heightened and
potentially lewd.

The framing of these sensations as "symptoms" draws on and further
embeds the belief that Asian cuisine is suspect into mainstream judgment.[17]
Krishnendu Ray argues that the overhomogenizing label of "ethnic food" supports the "unequal relationship between the self-proclaimed normative center
of the Euro-American imagination, its dominating institutions, and numerous
categories of others such as the foreigner, the tourist, the exile, the stranger,
the immigrant, etc., in a rich semiotic universe of slippery, relational self-
hoods and Otherness."[18] This Otherness of ethnic food emerges in discourse
but also in how the associated sensations of repulsion and distaste are so readily available for an eater to conjure forth. The *phantasmata*, the imprints of
such evocative sensory experiences, "provide the personal history that results
in assumptions, misidentifications, and the other types of perceptive error
that one might be drawn into."[19] In other words, the *phantasmata* themselves
might be factual in that they are a replica of an actual sensory experience, but
the current reality of these images shifts based on the interchange between the
individual's memories and the contours of the current situation, which leaves
room for misremembered experiences that can then be overlaid by problem-

14. Kwok, "Chinese-Restaurant Syndrome," 796.

15. Kennerly, "Getting Carried Away," 274.

16. Cohn, "Chinese Food Jinx."

17. See Sand, "A Short History of MSG." The MSG controversy was heightened by the
flurry of interest in possible chemical threats during this time fed by the publication of *Silent
Spring* in 1962. There were similar controversies over the use of the artificial sweeteners sac-
charin and cyclamate, although those have faded from public discourse.

18. Ray, *Ethnic Restaurateur*, 4.

19. Bubb, "Physiology of Phantasmata," 296.

atic ideological biases. Once we have digested the sensual, we have a pool of imaginative abstraction that can be retrieved as it aligns, or is made to align, with the current situation. The evoking of memory through phantasia is not grounded in an unerring facticity but rather a deliberate channeling of the sensorial through the present moment's emotional lens.

While this capacity can be used productively to invent rhetorical strategies, the chained logic of casting certain foods as inherently racialized and that racialization as the cause of negative bodily sensation demonstrates how phantasia can used in service of bad outcomes. The potential pleasure of "turning on" does not supersede the embedded belief of the perniciousness of MSG as a racialized, chemical contaminant. If bodily sensations are remembered as signs of direct bodily harm, the reasonable response is to focus on complete elimination of MSG and other ostensibly Asian ingredients from one's diet, which in turn reinforces existing beliefs that the consumption of Asian substances is to invite bodily destruction. Within such a rhetorical climate, cuisine becomes a prime area in which to exert one's self-control, producing a "well" body in opposition to the racialized body that craves MSG and other even more harmful substances.[20]

The casting of unfamiliar, non-Westernized foods as something to fear is entwined with proxemic assumptions about the danger from "over there" as emerging from the hands that make and minds that oversee. During the panic over lead contamination in children's toys from China, Mel Chen points out that the fear of the lead from "over there" overshadowed equally legitimate concerns about environmental lead poisoning in impoverished neighborhoods, mostly occupied by people of color.[21] The lead was made to stand in for "ideas of vulnerable sovereignty and xenophobia, ideas that demanded an elsewhere (or at least not interior North America) as their ground."[22] In the case of MSG, Chinese restaurants rhetorically function as an internal "there" that is poorer and dirtier than the norm of the white nation, evident in how "terms like 'abundant amounts' and 'appreciable quantities' were commonly used by researchers to differentiate between the use of MSG in Chinese and in other kinds of foods," that absolves the US of contamination via reliance on prior beliefs of deviance as belonging to the nondiscriminating outsider.[23]

20. See Morabito, "Racist 'Dirty Chinese Restaurant' Game" for an overview of how the video game company Big-O-Tree developed a game where players could choose to serve cat meat and to spit in patron's food. After controversy and claims from the company that the game was satire, the game was ultimately shelved.

21. M. Chen, *Animacies*, 155–56.

22. M. Chen, *Animacies*, 168.

23. Mosby, "'That Won-Ton Soup Headache,'" 143–44.

The perniciousness of the myth that MSG is harmful exemplifies the rhetorical power of casting phantastic experiences as indicative health measures. Despite the multiple instances of public scholarship on MSG discussing the lack of scientific evidence for its harm, those who believe they are sensitive or vulnerable to MSG explicitly ground their rejection of the scientific literature on their own bodily sensations that they remember from when they ate foods with MSG. This "thereness" is achieved via a reliance on phantasia's "invocation of magnitude," scaling a singular bodily experience upward into a representation of all possible racialized ills, inclining one's body toward disgust or fear even in the absence of direct harm.[24] Even if one believes that such sensations are psychosomatic or otherwise imagined, that does not diminish the attraction of being able to diagnose previously experienced unpleasant sensations via phantastic language. These articulations, in turn, redirect how people chose to speak of and act in relation to these foods or substances. The redirection of the conversation to individual sensation enables a continued elevation of the independent subject and a sidestepping of the racial inequities said subject inhabits.

This understanding of Asian food and Asian eating as bearing the sort of affective charge that leads to "turning on" is a result of its continued "exoticiz[ation] and romanticiz[ation]" in mainstream movies, cooking shows, and literature.[25] Eating an Other's food and being repulsed because of the extreme sensory experience is part of a long tradition of Othering Asian food through emphasizing the reaction of the non-Asian body. Such enactions of epideictic blame contour the limits of societal action through bracketing not only what actions are praiseworthy or blameworthy but what sensory reactions are allowable. Within a wellness-focused context where foods that evoke strong sensations are categorized as unhealthy, choosing high levels of sensation is to risk choosing forms of physical harm as well as moral behavior that falls outside the boundaries of this community. For example, the parade of television shows that market eating a variety of ethnic foods as a culinary adventure, such as *Bizarre Foods* and *No Reservations*, explicitly frame such food in terms of the show hosts' extreme reactions to eating it, both positive and negative. Due to the mediated form of these shows, the hosts' reaction exceeds the individual and comes to stand in for a broader "grammar of ingestion and avoidance" that the audience presumably aligns with.[26] Casey Ryan Kelly analyzes how these shows engage "the Other at the moment in which they might seem the most repellent, primitive, and backwards" through nar-

---

24. O'Gorman, "Aristotle's *Phantasia*," 28.
25. Xu, *Eating Identities*, 8.
26. Roy, *Alimentary Tracts*, 29.

rations of dishes like stinky tofu and durian fruit as "too putrid and foul" to finish eating.[27] Asian food, as a product that Asian bodies desire and cultivate, is used to signal the health risks of lower-class, nonwhite embodiment and to assure non-Asians of their status as modern individuals in the upper echelon. Status must be not only performed but felt.

The connection between personal taste and appetite as used in arguments around race and racial objects indicates how the social bonding power of affect in circulation can lead to "bodies becom[ing] increasingly closed down to alternative perspectives."[28] Affect is often framed as a continual process of becoming, but only focusing on its potential for flux fails to account for how affect can become attached to structures and organizations that prioritize immobility and inequity. Energy can be shunted into nonproductive or antiproductive situations; recirculation of stale air in a closed room is a flow that stifles. Within this "affective ecology" of praise and blame, racialized food is that which can always be judged as in need of rehabilitation or elevation.[29] Phantastic evocations of these histories can motivate assumptions about race or class absent overt rhetorical messaging.

For taste in particular, preexisting affective scaffolding for beliefs can even supersede direct bodily experience. Brian Massumi recounts an experiment in which people were given mislabeled flavors of jam or tea, yet they still convincingly argued for the superiority of the flavor they thought they were tasting, demonstrating how a "future sensation can be made to conform to a past sensation to which it is fundamentally different by force of expectation."[30] On the TV show *Ugly Delicious*, David Chang and historian Ian Mosby interviewed a focus group of people who believed they were susceptible to MSG.[31] After everyone ate the provided processed snacks, such as Doritos, Chang told everyone that all of the food contained MSG and asked them if they felt anything wrong. Even with this direct experience, several of them attempted to argue that their lack of symptoms meant that the dosage in Doritos was much lower than that in Chinese food. More than mere rationalizations, these contradictions demonstrate that the power of the sensory can be framed according to ideological assumptions that bypass whatever neutrality of sensation exists. Often, these tacit beliefs in sensory capacities as racialized remain unspoken, which makes it difficult to gauge their impact on interracial relations. What we see in the negative commentaries on Chinese

27. Kelly, *Food Television*, 31, 33.
28. Chaput, "Body as a Site," 97.
29. Rice, "Unframing Models."
30. Massumi, *Power at the End*, 24–25.
31. "Fried Rice."

and other cuisines is an expression of more overtly racist myths, for example "Asian food is unsanitary," funneled into preventative warnings about contact with ingredients or dishes in isolation.

Sensations, rather than purely a matter of the individual body, are made legible through patterned, socially normative understandings of the relationship between feeling and bodily states as either praiseworthy or blameworthy. Once this relationship has been established, it becomes possible to blame an object for being a cause of bodily ills while also absenting oneself from discussion of racial hierarchies or class separation through focusing on individual feeling. It is this sort of complex mediation that allows for the rhetorical positioning of oneself as a nonprejudiced individual because one still bears such strong desire for the object despite its seedy associations, and it also situates this rhetor as having gained expertise through trial and error, a move that also elevates them in terms of social capital. The level of detail that these rhetors use to develop a negative phantasia of the food object endows them with an implied expertise on said object that makes the eventual substitution of their version of the food object seem like a logical solution to this threat. Then the rest of us do not have to deal with the taint surrounding the racialized object *or* deign to explicitly discuss race and Asian America.

Such rhetorical sleight of hand, claiming certain expertise as race neutral for the purpose of discussing race-related objects, maintains separation between racial groups and their objects as objective realities. However, this recentering of whiteness is also inseparable from how social class is rhetorically framed according to consumption and production. The judgments of ethnic foods as cheap and dirty are recursive; this food must be dirty or contaminated because it is so cheap, but it also must be so cheap because the chefs are using dirty ingredients. While the assumption of grime might lend certain eating establishments a level of "authenticity," such judgments do not completely counterbalance the dominant understanding of Asian food as presenting a higher risk to one's health because of its dual associations with racial taint and lower-class crudeness. Phantastic descriptions are especially useful for separating out "high/low" versions of Asian food by mobilizing these tacit assumptions about race and class on the level of the individual, feeling body.

SENSATIONAL THREATS

In early 2019, there was a flurry of excitement and interest over the opening of a new restaurant, Lucky Lee, in New York City. Part of an informal trifecta of "Lucky" Asian restaurants opened by white restaurateurs in a single year

(Lucky Lee by Haspel, Lucky Cricket by Andrew Zimmern, and Lucky Cat by Gordon Ramsey), the anticipation turned sour due to several social media postings (now deleted) that contrasted the food at Lucky Lee's with other Chinese restaurants in ways that reinforced stereotypes of Chinese American food as inherently dirty and lesser than. An *Eater* article that documented some of the initial postings and backlash cites the deleted post as stating, "We heard you're obsessed with lo mein but rarely eat it. You said it makes you feel bloated and icky the next day? Well, wait until you slurp up our HIGH lo mein. Not too oily. Or salty."[32] In a follow-up interview with the *New York Times* aimed at mediating some of the accusations of racism, Haspel nonetheless doubled down on the focus on bodily feeling and stated that she created her restaurant so that "people who love to eat Chinese food and love the benefit that it will actually make them feel good."[33]

Rather quickly, those within the Asian American community and beyond shared Haspel's discourse and decried it as further evidence of racism in the restaurant business writ large. People took to Twitter, quoting Haspel's social media posts and pointing out the problematics of her marketing, merchandise, and branding. For example, many of the merchandise and branding materials used puns that required the parodying of stereotypical "broken" English and Asian accents, such as the sign that said "Wok in, take out" and dishes named "Egg Drop Mi-So Lucky Soup." Haspel also named the restaurant after her husband, whose first name is Lee, a choice that some felt was an attempt to mask the fact that they are both Jewish and do not have any direct cultural experience with Chinese food. In the multiple think pieces that circulated in response to the accusations of Chinese cuisine making everyone feel "bloated and icky," writers made explicit what was offensive about the rationales behind both the Instagram posts and the overall concept of Lucky Lee's. As writer MacKenzie Fegan put it, "I'm personally not opposed to people cooking the food of a culture to which they don't belong. I am, however, opposed to labeling the entire cuisine of a sprawling, diverse country as 'unhealthy' and suggesting that the half-million people of Chinese descent living in New York have all been waddling around, bloated and puffy-eyed, waiting for a white wellness savior."[34] Beyond the inaccuracy of Haspel's homogenization of Chinese restaurants, critics rightfully recognized the embedded assumptions about Asian embodiment as the result of and resulting in ignorant dietary choices.

---

32. Tuder, "New NYC Chinese Restaurant."
33. Otterman, "White Restaurateur."
34. Fegan, "We Don't Need."

In response to the number of complaints and rash of news coverage on the controversy, the Lucky Lee team deleted several of their most criticized Instagram posts and issued a new post with a lengthy apology. In Haspel's discussion of her phrasing of "bloated and icky," she directly addresses her role in choosing problematic language, particularly the statements on Chinese food as harmful, although she does not address the larger issue of cultural knowledge and expertise.[35] As with any public relations mishap-induced apology, Haspel performs the appropriate forms of remorse, coupled with statements about how it was not her/their intention to cause offense. She cites her New York City heritage in order to identify with her target audience of fellow New Yorkers, pointing out that "Arielle and Lee are both Jewish-American New Yorkers, born and raised. Similar to many other Jewish New Yorkers' diets, bagels, pastrami sandwiches and yes, American Chinese food, were big and very happy parts of their childhoods. New York is the ultimate melting pot and Lucky Lee's is another example of two cultures coming together. To us, this is a good thing." By positioning her use of Chinese food as part of her "melting pot" American heritage, Haspel affirms a similar ethos as audience members for whom Asian food is part of a nostalgic past, rather than a central present. Notably, she focuses on her experience as a nutritionist in terms of the broader wellness discourse community through directly referencing the cause-and-effect relationship she sees between food and physical feeling, relying on phantastic imaginings of the divide between "clean" and "dirty" food as clearly evident from an individual's physical reaction.

Yet even as Haspel affirms her positive feelings for Chinese food and yokes them to broader narratives of American assimilation and multiculturalism, she does not waver in her implicit critique of this cuisine's harmful aspects. She attempts to recenter the conversation around praise, not blame, by emphasizing the positive physical effects of her revised "gluten-free, dairy-free, wheat-free, corn-free, peanut-free" dishes. She achieves this positive tone by linking these positive bodily sensations with food that is explicitly revised away from a known racial origin. She states, "Chinese cuisine is incredibly diverse and comes in many different flavors (usually delicious in our opinion) and health benefits. Every restaurant has the right to tout the positives of its food. We plan to continue communicating that our food is made with high quality ingredients and techniques that are intended to make you feel great." In this statement, Haspel downplays the importance of cultural expertise or local specificity, employing a paratactic structure to align her own recipes with the "incredibly diverse" cuisine of China. She continues, emphasizing her res-

---

35. @luckyleesnyc, "The other day. . ."

taurant's "high quality ingredients and techniques that are intended to make you feel great." Epideictic rhetoric is effective in large part because of the contrast, either spoken or implied, between what is being praised and what is not. Here, the ingredients and techniques are framed as superior in their link to feeling "great," but the crux of this sentence is the Haspels' ostensible intentions for their customers' feelings. It is not just that attendees of the restaurant will come away renewed from eating the revised dishes but that they can rest comfortably knowing that the owners were spending their time and energy on caring about how its eaters feel. With this framing, owning an ethnic restaurant as a white business owner is recast as an intentionally safe space with notably higher moral values and, thus, health implications.

Haspel exemplifies how it is possible to express epideictic rhetoric toward a community and food while simultaneously reaffirming one's outsider point of view as central. She emphasizes her positive feelings toward Chinese food as something that was "a big and happy part" of her family life. Although one could take these statements as disingenuous, covering up her actual disdain for Chinese cuisine and culture, the more interesting question is how this overall positive, albeit superficial, orientation toward Chinese food can coexist with beliefs that it is also fundamentally unhealthy, perhaps actively harmful to one's body. Asking that question opens up room to explore how the tension between desire and repulsion that so often contours relationships with ethnic foods is part of a broader understanding of race/ethnicity as that which causes harmful effects to the nonminority body. The resulting relationship is one of mediating harm, either through strict scheduling (e.g., "cheat" days), abstention, or modification. The racialized food is allowable as long as it is controllable.

Haspel's attempted intervention in Chinese cuisine is rooted in broader discourses of wellness and "healthism" that center the interlocutor's bodily experiences as a valid form of authority; one's attunement to one's own body is framed not as an irrational focus on emotions but rather a careful gleaning of information from one's intensity of feeling. This worldview and associated lifestyle practices, sometimes labeled "healthism" and other times more generally understood as "wellness," becomes how one asserts one's worth as a responsible citizen who is capable of self-monitoring for life, constantly under "a mandate to identify dangers in order to control them."[36] Choosing to "control" one's health via constant self-surveillance is a means of maintaining one's status as a "responsible health citizen" who is praiseworthy for their carefully curated health choices, often through consuming certain products and avoid-

---

36. Crawford, "Health as a Meaningful," 403.

ing others.[37] Within this context, rhetorical strategies that focus on measurable steps to avoid danger or to increase feelings of health are especially persuasive in their promise of increased social agency; eating becomes "necessary for life-style, rather than sustaining life."[38] As measuring lifestyle ideals like "personal responsibility" and "good citizenship" is rather difficult, the presence of bodily sensations that are deemed healthy provides confirmation of the success of this wellness-focused life.

Wellness culture is embedded within the more extensive landscape of health and nutrition-related media that also centers feeling and sensation as a primary feature. For example, the current wave of social media influenc-ers was preceded by bloggers who jump-started the personal-testimony-to-fame pipeline. Healthy living blogs focus on food as salutogenic rather than as obesity-causing, and they tend to frame food and eating via "descriptions of the satisfying, sensory aspects of food—the smell, texture, visual appeal and especially the delicious taste of particular foods," as well as the "plea-sure in eating shared meals with friends and family."[39] While this focus on eating-as-pleasure is a needed contrast to the prevalence of fat-shaming and diet discourses, feeling within wellness discourse tends to manifest as abstract ideals that narrow the range of somatic normalcy to unachievable levels. In a study of diet detoxes, Katrine Meldgaard Kjær finds that instead of "focusing on a specific aesthetic or a medical concern with health, [the diet descrip-tions] focus on how the dieter will *feel* when following the program."[40] The focus on feeling as a direct indication of health that can be manipulated via intake and output supports the heightened focus on monitoring one's diet according to phantastic metrics of sensation. While not automatically harm-ful, such foci are easily rerouted to support abstracted ideal embodiments that rely on racial/racist understandings of physiological rightness. For example, the discourse surrounding the "obesity epidemic" insists upon "an irrefutable equivalence between thinness and self-control that extended to an equivalence between thinness and fitness for citizenship," all while ignoring inequities of access to healthy food and how norms for body size are themselves overlaid with racist assumptions.[41] The exclusionary epideixis of wellness culture pro-vides easy attachments for strains of thought derived from racist and classist hierarchies.

37. Derkatch, "Self-Generating Language," 154.
38. Cooks, "You Are What You (Don't) Eat," 95.
39. Rodney, "Pathogenic or Health-Promoting," 40.
40. Kjær, "Detoxing Feels Good," 708.
41. Biltekoff, *Eating Right in America*, 125.

THE WHITENESS OF "CLEAN" EATING

The dominant social identity of whiteness, as a normalizing orientation to the world and others, "constitutes normality and acceptance without [directly] stipulating that to be white is to be normal and right."[42] In addition to coded language and ranked tiers of symbolic capital, whiteness is maintained through tacit, affective cues that accrue into the limits around a properly consuming body. Although Chinese food is still immensely popular in the United States, the ubiquity cannot fully erase how it has been positioned at odds with a proper habitus, or how to be oriented toward eating healthy means to be oriented against an entire ethnic cuisine and the people that make and eat it. For example, eating Chinese food often signals that there are ruptures in one's bodily rhythms that have forced a temporary lapse into less healthy eating. In television shows across genres, the main characters eating Chinese food out of the recognizable white cardboard boxes connotes a lack of time or attention to eat a more proper, more nutritious meal.[43] The assumption that Chinese food needs to be improved in order to align with a healthy, American diet hovers in the background.

The focus on exorcising harmful substances, and thus harmful sensations, in arguments about dietary self-control quickly slides into denigrations of entire ethnic food traditions. For example, an article on the lifestyle site Goop, a site well known for its suspect understanding of wellness, proclaims that their versions of Chinese food are "not only better for you, but actually tastes better too." This article, titled "Better Than Takeout: Four Chinese Food Recipes to Make at Home," performs epideictic sleight of hand, assuming a monolithic unhealthy Chinese cuisine as the backdrop for the improved, "clean" version.[44] In "place of the MSG-laden, refined sugar-packed, gluten-heavy standard, we've clean-hacked some of our favorite takeout dishes, ditching the gluten and cheap cooking oil, and replacing it with quality ingredients and simple, flavorful sauces." The Goop writers draw on aesthetic language reminiscent of both fashion advice and food reviews to praise these new recipes for their ability to do "such a good job of satisfying takeout cravings" but in a healthier way. These recipes that "Hold the MSG" offer a route into a "clean-

---

42. Bonilla-Silva, Goar, and Embrick, "When Whites Flock Together," 231.

43. On the finale of the first run of the show *Sex and the City*, the character Charlotte is too distraught to cook and orders Chinese food. In response, her husband says that he "has something from China too" and pulls out a photo of the child they are hoping to adopt. This conflation of consuming chow mein and adopting a child was evidently played as a hopeful moment.

44. "Better Than Takeout."

hacked" reset. This framing of recipe intervention into an Other's culture as "improving on an unrefined, unsophisticated, incomplete, and, most crucially, unfashionable racialized form," characterizes all previous experiences with Chinese food as unhealthily impacting the readers' bodies.[45] Chinese food created by Chinese people is connected to a concrete moment in the reader's felt past, offering a version of the exotic primitive without any discussion of such. Rather, the emphasis is on the non-Asian reader as someone who occupies an assumed post-racial orientation toward all races and only wishes to propel forward into an already clean future. Left unstated is the amount of racial and financial privilege one must have in order to aspire to such levels of clean eating, as well as the time to practice and enact the knowledge embedded in even these modified recipes. The focus is on a clean food as an acontextual ideal.

Haspel's other work as a health-focused, "clean" food blogger exemplifies this orientation toward sensation as race and class neutral even as her recommendations enact oppositional views to qualities projected onto marginalized groups. Online blogs are one of the main digital spaces through which nutritionists, chefs, and other food-related entrepreneurs develop followings, and they are also a prime site for defining ethnic and cultural boundaries around food.[46] Haspel's discourse on health and wellness revolves around the belief that bodily feelings, specifically sensations that are related to eating, are the primary evidence of nutritional truth. A blog post titled "Food Trends: What Diet Is Right for my Body?" exemplifies this orientation toward sensation as the right metric for determining one's best health practices.[47] Throughout this post, Haspel encourages her readers to ground their food practices in the feelings that eating evokes in their body. She notes the challenge of figuring out "the right foods and exercise for your ultimate bod" and that multiple diets all promise "glowing skin and a fit body" or "energy, strength (and fertility)," stretching the definition of health to include qualities that enhance one's visual appearance and, therefore, social capital. The versions of health listed here conflate appearance, energy, and physical capacity (reproductive or otherwise), but all are given as future end results of one's dietary choices. The evidence for this projected future is a centering of personal sensation, as shown in a series of questions aimed at helping the reader figure out what diet is best for them, some of which are below.

45. M. Pham, "Racial Plagiarism," 74.

46. See Lopez, *Asian American Media Activism*, for a discussion of how Asian activists use blogs as a way to respond to harmful portrayals of Asians and Asian culture.

47. Haspel, "Food Trends."

- Does this way of eating fill me up? Do I feel energized when I wake up in the morning? How do I feel during the day? And how do I feel at the end of the day?
- Does this food satisfy all of my cravings?
- Do I feel deprived of any of my favorite foods? If so, what?
- How satisfied am I at the end of a meal? How satisfied am I at the end of the day[?]
- Am I excited to eat?

Haspel then states, "Remember that no matter what you choose to eat (and choose not to eat), a food philosophy shouldn't make you overthink or feel deprived or obsessive. Food should make you feel empowered, energized, and satisfied."

I detail her advice in order to point out how the equation of one's bodily reactions to food with future health and wellness results produces a negative space of possibility that can then be overlaid with problematic racial assumptions. The questions Haspel poses are rooted in a point of view that directly links health and nutrition to one's individual bodily feeling in terms of a spectrum of deprivation to satisfaction. Such a framework for conceiving of food replaces a checklist way of thinking about eating—for example, a food pyramid—but it does so by opposing the equally abstract states of deprivation and empowerment in ways that reflect class-based variance in access to nutritional resources and supplements. Any departure from these lofty sensory goals, including the common state of a lack of energy, easily slides into the negative category of "deprivation." The setup as all physical discomfort as the result of one's dietary choices provides a sense of control over one's embodiment through tying the range of tenable sensation to speculative categories, a rhetorical move that renders anything outside of these idealized goals as suspect. The bodily reactions to Asian food, rather than just being part of the physiological process of digestion, are then easily rendered as concrete causes of future diminished health.

Searching Haspel's blog for the terms "MSG," "Asian," and "Chinese" demonstrates how the centering of physical sensation in speaking of race and racialized objects does not negate racial bias. Instead, focusing on one's bodily reaction to said food as a provable metric of health can end up reenacting assumptions about sensation and race that reinforce such myths. In Haspel's posts where she denigrates MSG and other ingredients as (a) solely found in Asian American food and (b) inherently harmful through phantasia-laden remembrances, we see a broader positioning of ethnic food as inevitably causing bodily discomfort that is a signal of further future harm. In a post titled "Just Another Wellness Wednesday (Tamari)," Haspel argues for the inclusion of tamari sauce in her reader's diets rather than the more commonly used soy sauce.

> You know the morning after you go to your favorite chinese [sic] restaurant or sushi joint and you feel bloated, your eyes are puffy and your rings hardly fit on your fingers? It's probably due to the soy sauce you dipped your tuna roll in, which may be made of sugar, water, salt, caramel coloring, genetically engineered and pharmaceutically derived enzymes and preservatives. Many commercial producers of tamari soy sauce add ethyl alcohol as a preservative, while most organic tamari brands add a bit of naturally fermented grain alcohol derived from organic rice to preserve freshness.[48]

The structure of this central paragraph is familiar to many teachers of expository writing. The writer opens with a hypothetical question that introduces the topic by directly calling on the assumed experiences of the reader, both to form common ground and develop what is at stake. However, rather than root these shared assumed experiences in values or beliefs, Haspel directly calls on uncomfortable bodily experiences with water retention via calling on phantastic sense impressions, here blaming MSG for uncomfortable sensory experiences. The reader is meant to identify her negative experience of "feel[ing] bloated" and "puffy," so swollen that she is unable to wear jewelry the next day, as the direct result of visiting an Asian restaurant. Haspel hedges a bit in her linkage to soy sauce, noting it is "probably" the cause, but the overall direction of this setup "provides 'a kind of comparative seeing'" in which the contrast between one's typical bodily state and bloating is magnified and elevated to a symptom of possible pathology.[49] Once this link to potential disease is made in this imagining, Haspel can join these felt sensations to broader concerns about illness and the accumulation of harmful substances in the body. There is a quick jump from concerns over bloating to implicit blame in the framing of "genetically engineered and pharmaceutically derived" enzymes, blame that is underscored via her successive presentation of soy sauce and tamari as on opposite ends of the safe and healthy food spectrum.

The presentation of deracialized ingredients as stand-ins for racialized fears is only possible if the "responsible health citizen" of wellness culture is

---

48. Haspel, "Just Another Wellness Wednesday."
49. O'Gorman, "Aristotle's *Phantasia*," 28.

assumed to inhabit a white embodiment.[50] Haspel's description of the meeting of her own body and that of MSG as an exemplar assumes that cultural tourism is how her readers would encounter such a substance: at restaurants or sushi joints, never in the home. Within the wellness-based fear that one's body is "always at the edge of illness of failure and in need of external intervention to maintain function," the linking of this presumed cultural novelty to such explicit bodily sensation provides a concrete, Other source for these potential future failures.[51] Memory's weak understanding of causation is transformed into its suasiveness through phantasia, as these vivid descriptions can become infused with energy and emotion external to that original event. In Haspel's depiction of the morning after eating Chinese food, the uncomfortable bodily state of bloating is retroactively infused with active disdain for the now-understood-as-unhealthy ingredients being ferried into the reader's digestive system. Regardless of whatever actually caused the original sense of bloating—dehydration, overconsumption of alcohol, and so on—the thin layer of soy sauce is figured as a Trojan horse, trotting a range of chemical invaders into the reader's stomach. Absent a specific Other, the object that is in some way proximate to Asianness comes "to bear its own toxic racialization" in the eyes of the American consuming public.[52]

Haspel draws on a similar set of assumptions in her discussion of eating at restaurants in a post from 2014. In addition to categories like "Veggies" and "Breakfast," she tells her readers eating "Chinese" to explicitly ask for their dishes to be made according to a "clean" nutritional preference.

Ask for no msg: the stuff that makes you want to eat more and more and more. It's also the stuff that makes you super thirsty for the rest of the night! Chinese food is usually doused in processed oil and brown sauces which are full of sugar, so to play it safe . . . order some brown rice and fish or shrimp in a garlic sauce with lots of vegetables.[53]

The opening evocation of eating "more and more and more" resonates with the same fears of Asiatic devouring that inflect discourses around rat and bat eating. This sort of phantasia-based linkage offers resolve for bodily experiences that hover in the realm between official diagnoses and individual pains. Haspel opens by emphasizing sensations of hunger and thirst, but she then switches to language with embedded long-term health assumptions for

---

50. Derkatch, "Self-Generating Language," 154.
51. Derkatch, "Self-Generating Language," 147.
52. M. Chen, *Animacies*, 171.
53. Haspel, "Best Tips for Ordering."

the reader, cautioning them to "play it safe." Presumably, the reader might wish to avoid processed oil and sugar because of long-term health issues such as high cholesterol and diabetes. But these actual health issues are left unsaid, merely implied in the move from an immediate sensation like hunger and thirst to a state of being, chronic illness, that is not necessarily tangible in the same way. The use of phantasia to slide between a safe/harmful and immediate/long-term health binary conflates these points in a way that places Asian food into a category of eternal blame. This "bringing before the eyes," or perhaps "passing of plates under noses" exceeds a momentary issue of persuading someone to eat or not eat at a particular restaurant but extends more universally into how people approach the act of eating itself. If the plate that is supposedly laden with MSG is rendered as always harmful, encounters with the racial Other's food are always matters of risk mediation.

CONCLUSIONS

There are many reasons why centering individual sensation via listening to one's body in food culture is so persuasive. In a social context where access to medical care is unevenly spread across socioeconomic strata, as well as the ongoing issues with sexism and racism embedded in medical curricula, being able to gather and use knowledge about one's own body offers the promise of control over one's health and future. However, what we see in Haspel's and others' discourses is how there are recognizable patterns in these framings of existing biases against groups already marked as Other by class and/or race in the rhetorical casting of certain sensations as inherently negative. As Robert Crawford reminds us, the history of the professionalization of health is a history of eugenics in which "racial health" was the rhetorical basis for enacting state and social-level campaigns, such as sexual purity programs, against practices deemed unhealthy and unprofitable.[54] The positing of such framing as protective, warding off danger, masks how defining what is and is not healthy is part of a broader set of wedded racial and financial privileges that enable the maintenance of boundaries between "clean" and "unclean" eaters through a tightly curated range of allowable sensations. It is the same biopolitical urge to eliminate the unhealthy and contain the racialized, evident in the creation of racial ghettoes, that supports self-surveillance away from racialized sensations as best practice. Contemporary wellness discourse is not a-racial but

---

54. Crawford, "Health as a Meaningful," 406.

rather weighted with norms that prioritize defining health through a lens of bioracial equilibrium.

The rhetorical scaffolds that are regularly used in discourses surrounding diet and eating plans define healthy food in opposition to sensations and feelings that are attached elsewhere to more explicit arguments about the link between moral turpitude and racial minorities. Haspel and others ground their sense of cleanliness and health in the use of bodily phantasia in order to further their own ethos as nutritional authorities, but in doing so they reinscribe racialized and racist understandings of Asian food as an assaultive threat to bodily boundaries. These descriptions render the nutritional landscape as a naturally racialized terrain that one must navigate via reliance on self-contained physical experience, avoiding certain foods' ill effects that automatically translate into long-term health dangers. In setting up Asian food as the clearly overstimulating Other, one's "clean eating" is rendered even more comforting in its absence of physical sensation. In other words, the fraught navigation is the point, or, it only becomes possible to define clean eating in relation to the shadow of phantasia and the Other's potentially "dirty" impact on one's health.

Left unexamined, these beliefs about the links between personal responsibility, diet, and self-control provide rhetorical fodder for epideictic condemnation. In 2021, the defense team for the singer R. Kelly, who was accused of sexually assaulting and kidnapping numerous women, attempted to disqualify a victim's testimony by emphasizing that she had possibly consumed MSG via takeout Chinese food and was therefore mistaken or lying about her experiences of sexual abuse.[55] Fortunately, the defense failed, and R. Kelly was convicted. However, this moment points to the range of interconnected assumptions about food as an extension of Asianness that sows confusion and health risks into the otherwise healthy body. In this case, the assumption about Chinese food's ill effects on one's physicality and morality was wielded against Black female survivors of R. Kelly's predation. The strangeness of this moment, a defense attorney asking this woman if her story of being invaded by R. Kelly was actually a fever dream caused by an invasion of Asian food, demonstrates the often persuasive belief that racialized food is a danger best sussed out through attending to strange physical sensations.

Fortunately, there are a number of voices working against such insinuations, both in relation to the myth of MSG as harmful and the stereotype of Asian food as coequal with uncleanliness. Celebrity chef David Chang has used his platform to attempt to dispel the myths around MSG as part

---

55. Bekiempis, "R. Kelly's Lawyer."

of a broader mission to support Asian American chefs and foods. In January 2020, MSG producer Ajinomoto started the #RedefineCRS campaign to remove "Chinese restaurant syndrome" from Merriam-Webster's dictionary. Represented by celebrities such as chef Eddie Huang and TV presenter Jeannie Mai, the campaign succeeded in influencing Merriam-Webster to update the definition with the caveat of "dated, sometimes offensive."[56] In December 2021, the diet plan and company Whole30 removed MSG from their list of banned substances, citing the research on embedded racism in discourses around MSG as the reason for the change.[57] Social media campaigns such as #VeryAsian forward explicit statements of pride in Asian food and culture as necessary interventions. Beyond increased representation for Asian voices, these conversations recognize the rhetorical role of food to either foster social exclusion or self-actualization.

While it is incredibly important to call out anti-Asian sentiment where it inflects contemporary discourses surrounding food, this sort of work on discourse needs to be accompanied by attention to where these patterns are supported by tacit understandings of racially differentiated embodiments. Otherwise, the fears will shift into less overtly offensive verbiage, but the Asian body will remain understood as a source of unseemly stimulation and ill health. Close acquaintance with such bodies will still be seen as synonymous with potential contamination. As I will argue next, the belief that Asian bodies are always overstimulated, an inherent physicality that leeches into the foods they produce, is intertwined with the policing of Asian voices in discussions around race and inequality.

56. Ajinomoto, "#RedefineCRS."
57. Whole30 (@whole30), "NEW WHOLE30 RULE."

CHAPTER 5

"Too Sensitive" Speakers

The Limits on Asian Emotion in the Public Sphere

White people like to tell Asians how to feel about race
because they're too scared to tell black people.

—Margaret Cho, *Late Night with Seth Meyers*

The rise in anti-Asian violence that accompanied panic over the coronavirus demonstrates how the Asian body as a dangerous, deviant source of contamination is still an easy scapegoat. Yet in contemporary discourse, this historical formation of the Asian as "peril" is typically backgrounded in favor of an equally flawed understanding of Asians as part of the "model minority," notable for their intimidating intellectual and cultural superiority. The myth of all Asians as belonging to the "model minority" is usually traced back to a *New York Times* article written by sociologist William Petersen in 1966 in which he directly contrasted Japanese Americans' "Tokugawa values" with those of "the Negroes" and other racial groups, claiming that Asians were culturally superior as evidenced by their success in health and wealth.[1] The myth's focus on Asian cultures as naturally more predisposed to aligning with American values of humble diligence and academic achievement not only erases intra-Asian ethnic diversity but also maintains Asian Americans as always more Asian than American; their inherited culture grants them access to success in American society even as that presupposed cultural difference maintains their immutable foreignness.

Although the shift from fear to intimidation might sound like a positive as it seems to reflect a shift in the socioeconomic hierarchy, the underlying gut

---

1. Petersen, "Success Story."

orientation of the Asian figure as always causing upset to the US body politic is still present even in narratives of upward assimilation. When Asian achievement is recognized, it is figured as an attribute of "Asian roboticism" or other dehumanizing identifications that rely on an origin of "over there" as explanatory.[2] These contradictory expectations of awe and derision mean that Asians, especially within the aspirationally post-racial space of the United States, "are respected but disliked; the consequence of so-called positive stereotyping is that the other shoe always drops."[3] What I take up in this chapter is how the myth that all Asians are docile and accepting of their white-adjacent status is part of the same gut orientation toward Asian food and eating that validates whitened palates as superior to the tainted, unhealthy tendencies of Asians. The expectation for Asians to be silent and inexpressive by nature is tied to a belief in their contentment with, or at least, their lack of resentment for, the racial status quo. This results in rhetorical conditions where it is socially acceptable to exclude or shun Asian food and/or eaters under the guise of "clean eating," but Asian Americans are expected to be silent on the topic of one's place in racial hierarchies. To critique norms around food and eating, even when these norms are embedded in stereotypical assumptions, is to risk one's rhetorical authority being undermined with labels of "overemotional" and "too sensitive."

These expectations for emotional normativity are compounded further by ongoing gender stereotypes of Asianness as naturally occupying a "feminized position of passivity and malleability."[4] The Asian masculine has been derided as the realm of "efficient housewives" and as "effeminate, illegitimate, and divided" since the initial start of immigration to the US in the 1800s.[5] The "to-be-looked-at-ness" that marks the oversexualization of Asian femininity in the bedroom manifests as expectations of voicelessness outside of it.[6] Such stereotypes are, at their core, assumptions about a weakness of Asian corporeality that extends to the range of available emotions. To craft rhetoric as an Asian rhetor that directly confronts one's own racialization is to disrupt this expectation for robotic passivity.

On April 27, 2017, writer Bonnie Tsui penned an opinion article titled "Why Is Asian Salad Still on the Menu?" in the *New York Times* in which she attempts to demonstrate how the menu naming choices for salads at chain restaurants, for example the "Asian Emperor Salad," are indicative of outdated

2. Bui, "Asian Roboticism," 111.
3. Bow, "Racist Cute," 44.
4. Okihiro, "Perilous Frontiers," 199.
5. Eng, *Racial Castration*, 210.
6. Kang, *Compositional Subjects*, 12.

stereotypes of Asian individuals.[7] This one opinion article generated over six hundred commented responses and a flurry of response articles on other news platforms (such as *The Daily Wire*), most of which mocked Tsui's argument as "too sensitive," a fetishizing of authenticity, and/or anti-diversity. I analyze the article and the controversy it produced in order to illustrate how the expectation for docility of Asian feelings in discourse is but the echo of the strain of Asian embodiment that renders the "model minority" myth persuasive and Asians the "safe" race; civic participation is reduced to cooking and serving, rather than thinking and analyzing. The Asian body that expresses discomfort with the contours of racial life is actively disrupting social hierarchies for no apparent reason and therefore needs to be tamed by a perspective that purposefully decenters the emotional and embodied. The available rhetorical stance for Asianness is self-effacing and lacking subjectivity, traits assumed to be naturally more feminine in opposition to the self-determined, white Western voice.

In this chapter, I analyze how the fears and distrust of the Asian eater are negotiated in discourse that centers not the Asian body but a more abstract discussion of the model minority's role in a post-racial society. More specifically, I parse how the responses to Tsui legitimate a continued ignoring of racial issues surrounding Asian American identity through displacing attention to ethnic variety onto European ethnic groups. To illustrate this cognitively dissonant rhetorical stance, I discuss how the expectations for emotional performance that accompany the model minority stereotype are embedded in broader assumptions about the intersection of race and gender. I then analyze how commentators who reject Tsui's view of Asian ethnic specificity do so through the yoking of two topoi, hypersensitivity and ethnic authenticity, in mini narratives of "overcoming" emotional attachment to one's own ethnic background in order to affirm the rightness of American assimilation, even as doing so also reembeds attention to European American traditions as dominant. Tsui, as a representative of Asian American females, is violating tacit expectations for "model minority" abasement and the feminine role of emotional server rather than expresser. Just as the figure of the Asian-as-bat-eater "disciplin[ed] and normaliz[ed] subjects *away from*" deviant race and orality during and after the initial COVID pandemic, the figure of the overexcited Asian is a rhetorical straw man used to normalize performances of the tamed, assimilated feminine figure that proclaims post-racial values as the ultimate

---

7. In her stand-up show *Revolution*, the comedian Margaret Cho satirizes the layers of ambiguity in the label "Asian Chicken salad," notably performing affront at receiving a salad with no "crispy wonton crunchies."

good.[8] Via these topoi, Tsui's concern about treating Asian Americans as a racial monolith is taken up as a distraction from the sort of multicultural harmony found in sharing meals, and these arguments are wielded by Asians and non-Asians alike in exhortations for Tsui to fall in line with the image of the demure, passive Asian.

The expectation for "a politics of assimilation in which foreign excess must be translated into easily digestible and overtly domesticated signs of difference for it to be palatable" is evident in the stereotype of all Asian food as too spicy for white palates, but the case of Tsui's article demonstrates how such expectations manifest in the tamping down of discourse on racial difference.[9] The desire for multicultural contact via food does not subvert privilege differentials but rather masks how the production of that desire is the result of power inequities that assume constellations of bodies, fixed into unequal relations. Eating an Other's food is held up as exemplary of a neutral free-market exchange among equals, and any attempt to clarify the roles of race and ethnicity in global foodways threatens the distribution of this cultural capital.

DELEGITIMIZED EMOTIONS OF ASIAN BODIES

Emotion, as a rhetorical act, is always tied to overlapping expectations for the performance of race and gender. Public display of emotion, in particular, is constrained by "hegemonic social norms" for the limits of dis/allowable behavior.[10] Intense emotions, such as anger, when expressed by bodies that fall outside of the white, male, Protestant norm, have historically been diminished and delegitimated, even when that anger results from social injustice and exigencies. Eguchi and Asante point out how the hegemonic forces of heteronormativity and white supremacy intertwine to produce acceptable "volumes" for conversations around race, often with shame-based silencing of minority bodies that speak of dominant norms, much less critique them. The assumption of the Asian figure as always feminized, and therefore silent on social issues like racial inequality, buts up against the "power of White gay normativity" and produces paradoxes in the available performances of queerness.[11] Crucially, the feminization required for the Asian figure to be desirable is predicated on silence around race. When speaking of his dating history with "three non-White men," one of Eguchi's partners responds with, "I do not think that

8. Puar, *Terrorist Assemblages*, 38.
9. Mannur, *Culinary Fictions*, 186.
10. Winderman, "Anger's Volumes," 330.
11. Eguchi and Asante, "Disidentifications Revisited," 178.

people really care about race as much as before. Don't be so negative."[12] The reception of speaking of race as automatically not just taboo but as an emotional violation that reflects badly on the speaker's ethos speaks to how the projections of feminized embodiment tacitly demand silence around the topic of race.

Many of the responses to Tsui's article expressed this same combination of negation and critique. No, you aren't seeing anything, but also, why would you bring it up? I am less concerned with whether these comments are representative of how all Asians are viewed in the US and more with how a more feminine, passive positioning is seen as a legitimate rhetorical means to mediate the competing, overlapping, but never fully positive attributions projected onto Asian Americans. Recent controversies such as GamerGate and #MeToo have demonstrated how hostile online environments can be to marginalized speakers. Even within the "third place" of the internet where users "can reconstitute themselves as 'people' apart from their kinship and work networks" and negotiate the tensions amidst personal identity, racial stereotype, and external pressures, these affordances of the digital overlap with racialized expectations of emotional passivity and foreclose avenues of rhetorical agency for the Asian speaker.[13] Online spaces can provide room for the generation of commonplaces and strengthening of racial identity, as with Black Twitter, but absent a collectivity of coidentified voices, the public nature of such forums is structurally weighted toward supporting normative expectations for the performance of race and gender.[14] When looking at online forums, one is not getting a representative sample of beliefs but rather witnessing the concentration of existing attitudes that hold persuasive weight in the public sphere. The hyperbolic responses that negatively describe Tsui's article with phrases like "The inanity, the sheer, breath-taking inanity" (manta666, April 29, 2017), "Ludicrous nonsense" (Tjohn, April 29, 2017), and lacking "emotional strength" (spg, April 27, 2017) are reflective of broader assumptions about the appropriate cartography of emotion in relation to racial demographics.

These responses to Tsui are not just rude but draw on rhetorical topoi, also known as commonplaces, which are the "stock epithets, figures of speech, exempla, proverbs, sententiae, quotations, praises or censures of people or things, and brief treatises on virtues and vices" that are used to develop one's argument in a culturally relevant and appealing way.[15] For example, cultural touchstones like "#MeToo" and "being woke" can be used as an assumed

---

12. Eguchi and Asante, "Disidentifications Revisited," 178.
13. Brock, "'Who Do You Think You Are?,'" 17.
14. Florini, *Beyond Hashtags*.
15. D'Angelo, "Evolution of the Analytic *Topoi*," 54.

shared point of knowledge to bolster one's rhetorical credibility as a community member in crafting an argument. Christa Olson argues that topoi bear rhetorical power because they operate through "indexing and incorporating available assumptions about the bodies they reference."[16] In other words, these "storehouses of social energy" that "organiz[e] our lifeworlds" are always in tacit conversation with existing stereotypes about ways of being in certain bodies.[17] These inventional tools are not neutral bearers of argument but also inform and maintain certain bodily relationships, and hierarchical proximities, as normal. In thinking through how racist and racialized attitudes lurk in discourse, a key place to look is at how topoi are used to frame bodies and emotions as operating together in patterned ways.

The meaning of "authenticity" changes depending on one's vantage point. If one is searching for one's cultural identity after a diasporic migration, "authentic" might mean navigating one's connection to historical and geographical origins in tandem with experiences in one's new home.[18] If one is superficially curious about cultural practices of the Other, "authenticity" might be closer to a synonym for "quality" or "flavor." Something that is authentic is presumed to emerge from an "unbroken arc from a historical origin to the present manifestation of a cultural tradition."[19] For many "foodies" who view cultural heritage as accessible through consumption of a product, authenticity is "the White Whale of modern epicurism" that must be sought after and collected.[20] The ambiguousness of this topos and its reliance on perception means that it can be rhetorically deployed to increase or decrease distance between self and other, gaining ethos through proximity to or distance from the "authentic." As we will see in the responses to Tsui's article, the commentators primarily discuss their experiences with a *lack* of ethnic authenticity in order to demonstrate the moral superiority of moving past the search for the fiction of the authentic. This enables a claim of radical inclusion even as this metric is based on experiences of "moving past" experiences with European American ethnic groupings, identities that are arguably closer to the racially expected norm than those of Asian Americans. In this framework, "authentic" and "factual" become synonymous, which means that focusing on one's distance from or proximity to ethnic authenticity is a rhetorical strategy that allows people to claim affinity with difference and/or negate difference's impact on social life as is needed.

16. Olson, "Performing Embodiable Topoi," 303.
17. Cintron, "Democracy and Its Limitations," 101–2.
18. Clary-Lemon, "'We're Not Ethnic.'"
19. Tippen, *Inventing Authenticity,* 37.
20. Ku, *Dubious Gastronomy,* 37.

Commentators balance their own relationship to ethnic authenticity with the topos of hypersensitivity. Specifically, they project onto an imagined, "overemotionalized racialized subject" who is unable to exert the self-control required to fall in line with white norms for seemliness and style.[21] The societal-level tendency to label those who speak of race as overly emotional is part of the broader project of "racial sedimentation," a "technology of racism" that relies on unexamined "common-sense logics of interpretation" for emotional comportment.[22] Hypersensitivity is a commonplace that shrinks the issue of racism down to a matter of individual feelings, rather than being something that exists within and also shapes language and society. This topos relies on a tacit understanding of the neoliberal citizen as a self-contained unit, emotionally unaffected by outside influence and rigorously prepared for all arguments with rationality. In operation, the references to hypersensitivity simultaneously reinforce existing codes for unacceptable gendered behavior, specifically the too-"shrill" woman who speaks openly of her emotional feelings, and reinforce expectations that the "model minority" express gratitude serenely. The intersectional existence of an Asian female writer is a vulnerable site from which to voice discontent.

A gut orientation toward Asianness that expects emotional censorship to maintain model minority status is one that expects Asian food to remain in the realm of "culinary curiosities."[23] Or, the same logics that demand Asian Americans fit the model minority mold are those that rhetorically frame Asian food as a delicious supplement to American life, rather than as a collection of cuisines with rich cultural history forged at the intersection of immigration, globalization, and personal taste. Asianness is understood as "something that can assimilate *quietly* and *subtly* into the U.S. culinary landscape," just as Asian American belonging within the white sphere of the US is contingent upon modification of bodily and emotional comportment.[24] What we see in the below exchanges are examples of how the overlapping racialized and gendered expectations for the Asian figure to remain passive and assimilable are put forth to delegitimize arguments and identities.

THE POST-RACIAL FLAVOR OF ASIAN SALAD

Tsui's *New York Times* article explores the vagueness of post-racial discourse through calling attention to the nonspecific signifiers on chain restaurant

21. Ngai, *Ugly Feelings,* 91.
22. Houdek, "Racial Sedimentation," 281.
23. Xu, *Eating Identities,* 8.
24. Mannur, "Model Minority Can Cook," 85, emphasis added.

menus that gesture toward a universal Asianness, rather than attend to any geographic or ethnic specificity.[25] As Tsui puts it, "In the weird cultural geography of the casual-restaurant menu, half-century-old jokes about Asians and long-discarded terminology jostle up against chicken tenders and nacho plates." She argues that dish titles such as "Oriental Chop Chop" are synecdoches for how Asian Americans are often viewed in mainstream discourse: unified in geography, intention, and abilities. Yet the salads are neither named in a way that offers them full assimilation into the American cuisine nor given ethnic or geographical nuance. Rather, they are always still marked as Asian in a sloppy, overgeneralizing manner. Even as Tsui argues that the "broad, generic terminology used to refer to an entire continent" needs to be reconsidered, she also states that her wish is not that these salads disappear from menus altogether. Rather, she understands "that it's possible to feel fondness for a dish that is deeply inauthentic and I don't resent that one bit. It has become its own thing. Just don't call it Mr. Mao's Chicken Surprise."

Tsui's main claim is that the ongoing acceptance of such decontextualized cultural references in food naming is part of the larger normalization of boundaries between whiteness and the margins in everyday linguistic practices, a gut orientation toward Asianness as an ever-renewing novelty. As she puts it, "The language of the Asian salad is revealing of the dangers of bland, disembodied generalization: When you fail to see countries and cultures as discrete entities, what kind of consideration could you be expected to give to individual people?" Krista Ratcliffe points out that the cultural logic of multiculturalism is that one that lauds superficial differences, such as food, while leaving broader racist views intact.[26] In the cases that Tsui describes, the refusal of ethnic nuance is a manifestation of this sort of superficial engagement that leaves intact racist understandings of racialized embodiment and practices. For example, the "Chicken Asian Chop Chop" salad from the Houlihan's Restaurant chain draws on an onomatopoeic representation of the hand movements that supposedly represent the prominent use of heavy cleavers in Chinese cooking. Yet this specific marker of cultural knowledge is reduced to a repetitive hand motion, robotic in intonation. The implied Asian body is one of efficiency and speed but no depth.

Tsui's article attempts to check this ongoing misrepresentation through calling out "the wide-ranging, 'all look same' stereotypes of Asian culture." Although a seemingly small example of menu items, it is the accumulation of these sorts of microaggressive moves within from the public sphere that

---

25. Tsui, "Why Is Asian Salad."
26. Ratcliffe, *Rhetorical Listening*, 15.

both impacts "the psychosocial understanding within racialized communities" and "shapes the psychosocial understanding of those who interact with members of racialized communities and those who ultimately influence policies, structures, and institutions that affect these racialized communities."[27] In other words, these everyday representations create feedback loops where those with the rhetorical and legal power to represent racialized communities in the public sphere are subtly, over time, taught to conceive of and interact with Asian Americans as a monolithic Other, and the resulting representations also reinforce for Asian Americans what the correct way of enacting their racial identity is supposed to look like. Cathy Park Hong speaks to how these expectations are often internalized and manifest in how Asian Americans move through the world: "Asians take up apologetic space. We don't even have enough presence to be considered real minorities. We're not racial enough to be token. We're so post-racial we're silicon."[28] To act in a different way from these majority representations is to invite cognitive and psychological dissonance, as evidenced by the high volume of self-identified Asian commentators who directly attacked Tsui and her argument.

Despite her concluding emphasis that it is not "authenticity" but naming practices that are problematic, the largest area of uptake in the comments centers on the supposed binary of authentic/inauthentic as evidence for Tsui's hypersensitivity. For example, Tsui's article was denigrated on a number of conservative websites, such as the *Daily Wire,* the *Blaze,* and the *Resurgent,* where authors and commenters inveighed against this "political correctness" run amok. These varying responses to Tsui's work echoed and amplified the *New York Times* commentators' view that this is just another "ridiculous thing deemed racist."[29] Notably, multiple responses centered on Tsui's hypothetical question of whether or not she is taking the issue too seriously as a means of calling out what she sees as "casual racism." Tsui asks, "Am I taking this too seriously? The casual racism of the Asian salad stems from the idea of the exotic—who is and isn't American is caught up wholesale in its creation." Even though Tsui never uses the word "sensitive" as a descriptor, even in jest, many commentators framed her use of the word "serious" as a direct indication of her overall "sensitivity." For example, KRQ wrote, "Respectfully, this is hypersensitivity writ large. Part of the strength of America is its defining ability to incorporate and integrate the culture of others. The name simply refers to the use of 'exotic' ingredients. As best I can tell, no one has ever named a salad with malignity in mind" (April 27, 2017). In a *Daily Wire* article, the

---

27. V. Pham and Ono, "'Artful Bigotry and Kitsch,'" 176.
28. Hong, *Minor Feelings,* 7.
29. Prestigiacomo, "New York Times Labels Salad Racist."

author performs a similar interchanging of Tsui's words with ascribed emotional intent.

> "Am I taking this too seriously?" she asks.
> YES!
> But there is no reflection upon the rhetorical question; Tsui simply doubles-down on the sensitivity.[30]

The shift from "serious" to "sensitive" is a rhetorical shift from a societal-level issue to a matter of personal upset, from epistemological gravity to ontological fragility. This uptake and reframing of Tsui's argument emphasizes emotion as detracting from her ethos as a rational rhetor; to ask such a question, Tsui must be operating from a bruised affective state that hyperreacts to a perceived insult. She is framed as using the sort of "exaggerated emotional expressiveness" that "seems to function as a marker of racial or ethnic otherness in general."[31] This small moment of word substitution positions Tsui as operating from an illogical, overly emotional point of view, which in turn enables commentators to successfully frame their own ethos as more logical and thus more superior. Commentator Stephen Maniloff states that the article is "layers upon layer of nonsense . . . We should all shed a tear. . . . Of Laughter," and many commentators proclaimed some version of "Get a life" or "Get over it" (April 27, 2017). More than snarky dismissals, these comments are calls for Tsui to occupy a substantially different emotional relationship to her chosen topic. Rather than take it so seriously, so sensitively, she needs to recalibrate her emotional barometer so that she too can laugh at the triviality of salad naming despite the racial stereotyping and move on.

The focus on Tsui's sensitivity is part of a gut orientation that necessitates ethnic cultures and foods exist at a distance from the normative white center. Even in positive descriptions where these foods are described as a near-mythical prize for the enlightened adventurer, the valorization of travel and/or other labor to find such foods is indebted to the same distancing function embedded in accusations of rat or bat eating. In this orientation toward a racial Other's food, one's performance of the appropriate emotional orientation, an eagerness for contact with the distant multicultural, becomes the most important measurement of one's ethos as a diversely minded eater. Yet this expressing of deep love for the variety of foods, authentic and nonauthentic alike, dodges the question of how judgments of authenticity in an Other's

---

30. Prestigiacomo, "New York Times Labels Salad Racist."
31. Ngai, *Ugly Feelings*, 94.

culture are usually centered in middle-class, Western traditions of hygiene, ingredients, and preparation. Asian salads are diminished with names like "chop chop salad," while even a visit to the Olive Garden requires differentiating between terms like "parmigiano," "alfredo," and "ziti." Tsui's critique of the choice of salad name strikes such a nerve because it is also a critique of the narratives, usually so feted, that pose Asian food as an unchanging foil to more elevated Western cuisine.

The attention to Tsui's level of sensitivity also intersects with broader understandings of affective appropriateness when discussing sensitive topics like race and representation. The standards for "commonsense" reactions to controversial topics is deeply entangled with dominant "regimes of perception" that prioritize emotional neutrality and define appropriate ways to perform one's connection to one's embodiment.[32] The rancor toward Tsui is part of this larger affective regime that expects the minority body to be hyperemotional and preemptively regulates the range of available channels for those emotions. In order for "too sensitive" to count as a legitimate critique, there must be a baseline level of sensitivity that appears as appropriate to the majority of citizens in its apparent nonracial neutrality. For example, despite Tsui's claiming of a minority identity as a "Chinese-American," several comments reference Tsui's hypersensitivity as an indication of privilege that strips her of the right to comment about social ills.

> I want this woman's life. I want a life so free of stress and problems that I can work myself into such a lather about salads and their names, that I rant about it for twelve paragraphs, and get it published in the New York Times. I guess if everything in this world offends you, the only solution is to never leave your house, and have no contact with the outside world whatsoever. For heaven's sake, get a thicker skin. (td, April 28, 2017)

The hypersensitive topos enables a move to a generalized ethics that frames the Asian female author, "so free of stress and problems," as shutting herself off from the world in a way that opposes multicultural values. The intensity of this reaction to Tsui's attempt to discuss tacit racism is brought on by a perceived violation of the unspoken agreement that since Asian Americans are "next in line" to be white, talking about racial hierarchies is to be ungrateful for one's relatively high position. Even speaking about a small issue with race

---

32. Panagia, *Political Life of Sensation*. See also Williams, "Toward a Theorization of Black Maternal Grief" for discussion of how Black women, particularly mothers of murdered children, are expected to stifle their personal grief and perform a sort of noble victimhood when in the public eye.

dynamics in the US invites this sort of aggressive response because the presumed financial and social privilege of being Asian American is expected to outweigh consideration of race.

One comment by Steve B. explicitly foregrounds his understanding of the appropriate emotional relationship to multiculturalism as a counterargument to Tsui. This comment fits the typical profile of a comment on a *New York Times* article in terms of tone (general politeness), length and complexity (multiple sentences, three paragraph breaks), and evidence-based argumentation reminiscent of the upper-middle-class education that marks the expected *New York Times* readership. Steve B. uses the space in order to critique the authenticity of the food he ate as a tourist, but he does so in a way that centers his appropriate level of enthusiasm for this "inauthentic" food. To start, he appeals to his own geographical upbringing—"I am from Quebec"—and then details an experience he had eating poutine in Pune, India.

> I am from Quebec. The hallmark of our popular cuisine is arguably the poutine—French fries, cheese curds and gravy.
>
> One day, I visited Pune, India. The restaurant was selling a "French Canadian Poutine" (as if there were other types of poutine, or French Canada couldn't be subdivided in two or more societies). Gave it a try. It did not really taste the way it was supposed to, starting with the wrong cheese being used. But it was still decent and good.
>
> As a native, I did not take offense the Indian cooks did not import the right type of cheese straight from Quebec or hired a cook from home. Sure, not authentic, but no less authentic than a pizza in America (those of you that traveled to Italy know what I am talking about). It just felt nice that half a world away someone took the time to acknowledge, albeit imperfectly, where I am from and try to offer a bit of an international culinary experience to locals.
>
> In othee [*sic*] words, I am sorry to say the author is a bit too sensitive. (April 29, 2017)

This comment encapsulates the mix of contradictory attitudes that emerges from a centering of Western standards for emotional sensitivity when discussing race and ethnicity. Ironically, Steve B.'s focus on the proper emotional performance of multiculturalism causes him to overlook possible *stasis* between his and Tsui's perspectives. Tsui is calling out the lack of attention to ethnic specificity with the overgeneralizing term "Asian," while Steve B. is also concerned with the use of "French Canadian" as an overgeneralized label. Yet while Steve B. finds the poutine "not authentic," he still congenially praises the cooks for trying to "offer a bit of an international culinary experience to locals." Steve B. explicitly posits his ability to "not take offense" at the non-purity of this ethnic dish and enjoy the meal as evidence of a broader, more culturally embracing ethic that he judges as missing from Tsui's writing. Although he assumes a pure enough Quebecian status in order to judge other poutines, he quickly shifts focus to his ability to enjoy nonauthentic food in a foreign country as evidence for what a secure ethnic identity looks like. Yet this performance of non-offense is built at the expense of those cooks in Pune, India, and their failure to exactly reproduce poutine; the "imperfection" of the resulting dish is simultaneously not worth becoming angry over and usable as an illustration of the continued comparative primitivity of Asian attempts to mimic the West.

To an extent, the arena of food is the perfect set-up for this sort of rhetorical substitution of ethnicity for race. As Jennifer Ho points out, "Food is usually thought of as being ethnic rather than racially specific. Restaurants in the United States generally serve cuisine tied to an Asian nation (pan-Asian fusion restaurants notwithstanding), and the way that we talk about the Asian ethnic food that we cook and consume is through ethnic-national markers."[33] The shorthand that has evolved around food culture in the United States creates sympathetic space, ironically enough, for those who feel that discussing race is a bridge too far. In line with this logic of multicultural eating, the commentators cite their own experience with crossing *ethnic* boundaries as evidence of a proper attitude toward *race* and authenticity. A rhetorical effect of this paradigm is a facile reduction of difference, a flattening out of the historical and national events that have shaped societal perceptions of cultural traditions and associated epistemologies. Ethnicity is a murky space that allows for the simultaneous recognition of difference via a reduction of that difference to an offshoot of the dominant group's cognitive map of the world.[34] Within a US context, the layering of this attention to authenticity positions the eater of multiculturalism as an example of American exceptionalism, the enlightened subject who eagerly seeks engagement with the Other beyond US borders. Such framing is a stark rhetorical omission that glosses over the struggles over Third World liberation, immigration to the US, and the echoes

---

33. Ho, "Acting Asian American," 306.

34. To define ethnic or racial authenticity as fixed ignores the multiple historical forces and events that render culture itself ever-changing. In the blog for his Taco Literacy class, Steven Alvarez draws parallels between the syncretism of colonial religion (the Virgin Mary) and local practices (the goddess Coatlicue) and the development of tamales; globalization means there is more access to multiple types of tamales/religion, but the tendency is to narrativize the most familiar version as the most authentic.

of Western colonization that are particularly salient aspects of identity within the broader Asian American community.

The commentators like Steve B. that focus less on hypersensitivity and more on their love of other cultures and even failed ethnic authenticity use a tone that is celebratory of food as a multicultural bridge, and they explicitly use this more positive tone as a way to position themselves as ethically superior to Tsui in their attention to difference.

> I love other cultures. When I went to Japan, I ate at local "workers district" hole in the wall eateries. When I was in Russia, I ate blini at a vendor stand in Bauman Street, Kazan. If you have the chance, certainly take advantage of the opportunity but don't reject an adapted cuisine or feel insulted by it just because it doesn't represent authentic ethnic cuisine because it's that or nothing. (J.I.M., April 28, 2017)

Although online discussions about race are often marked by negative views of minority groups and the use of slurs and negative exaggerations, perhaps due to the "cloak of relative anonymity" that can be used as "a cover for racial hate groups," the comments on Tsui's article are performed as reasonable and rational, even complimentary of certain ethnic attributes.[35] Yet even as they perform a sort of rational orientation to valuing ethnic diversity, they also still avoid engaging with Tsui's argument by framing engagement with difference as a binary of "that or nothing." Tsui's attention to ethnic specificity is taken as a crude obsession with authenticity that distracts from multicultural unity. The unruly Asian body that dares to disturb norms of post-raciality just needs to get past its insulted feelings and assimilate to this more enlightened view that embraces diversity. In addition to the brief comments that used hypersensitivity as a rejection of the entire article's premise, such as "Well, aren't we sensitive. Even the salad is wacist now," many of the longer comments coupled hypersensitivity with explicit references to how their own European ethnic background has been misrepresented. For example, commentator J opens with an appeal to their own European ethnic identity and progresses through a discussion of their own travel experiences in Asia, concluding with the claim that their ability to achieve emotional equilibrium over such misrepresentations is the appropriate emotional response. Ethnicity, particularly European American ethnicities, are still the safest territories in which to try to discuss difference within a purportedly post-racial rhetorical landscape that sees explicit discussion of race as threatening to a multicultural gloss of harmony.

35. Bargh and McKenna, "Internet and Social Life," 584.

As an Italian:

You are taking these things too seriously.

American cuisine has appropriated Italian ingredients and labels all sorts of things as Italian even though Italian people don't touch them.

There are many delicious cuisines in Asia. When in Korea I went to an "Italian-Korean" restaurant called Mad For Garlic where they sold all sorts of Korean riffs on Italian dishes. The restaurant was filled with faux-Italian tchotchkes. I was served a pasta dish that was garlicky. Instead of cheese I was given dried seaweed. It was not Italian food but I enjoyed it and was happy my Korean friends took me there.

Food is a great way to connect with people. These ridiculous accusations of "cultural appropriation" should be dismissed out of hand. "Inauthentic" is not a bad thing. Imitation is the finest form of flattery. (April 27, 2017)

Within the comment itself, the boundaries the writer sets around race and culture fluctuate as needed to prove that thinking about the relationship between race, ethnicity, and food in the way that Tsui is doing is to reify racist views of the world. So, J opens with a definitive statement about their own ethnic, perhaps cultural, identity and then provides a counterexample to Tsui via their own experience as an Italian in Korea. Within their example, they juggle the murky line between race and ethnicity, starting with a comment on food in "Asia" but then quickly reducing that broader category to one experience in a single country. In their own tourist experience in a racial context where Italians are the minority, this author details the multiple ways that the Korean chefs got Italian food "wrong" but then actively emphasizes the emotional pleasure they gain from interacting with even nonauthentic food as a way of modeling what an appropriate, nonsensitive way of interacting with racial Others' food should look like. This final emphasis on social connection thus not only is a personal judgment of Tsui but also moves toward an ethical argument that Tsui's "ridiculous accusations" are actually preventing social connection with others. The prescription for Tsui and others like her is to not focus on the details of authenticity but rather on the emotional motives of those preparing it.

bell hooks describes this emphasizing of one's desire for the Other as a more covert expression of racist logics. Often, people who proclaim a love for other cultures "do not see themselves as perpetuating racism. To them the most potent indication of that change is the frank expression of longing, the open declaration of desire, the need to be intimate with dark Others. The point is to be changed by this convergence of pleasure and Otherness."[36] In J's

36. hooks, "Eating the Other," 24.

case, they are able to extract emotional enjoyment from their time in Korea, and they presume a similarly positive engagement from the Korean chefs who intended to "flatter" their Italian customers. The points that Tsui raises about power differentials in the cooking and selling of another race's food products are subsumed under a belief that all parties in these cases of cooking and selling food gain the same level of enjoyment from such an exchange. One's level of positive affect toward the prepared or eaten food stands in for a more substantive discussion of power differentials or cultural capital. This reliance on a unnuanced understanding of multicultural contact enables these commentators to distance themselves from any perceived "white" cultural pride that might threaten the presumed social harmony of a post-racial society while also claiming their own ethnic specificity. Thomas K. Nakayama and Robert L. Krizek describe the dominance of whiteness, where to be white, absent color, "is considered natural rather than cultural," a rhetorical move that "elides any recognition of power relations embedded in this category."[37] In these comments, the emphasis on ethnicity, rather than race, enables these commentators to define sensitivity as part of a previous era's racial inequity rather than as part of current orientations toward difference.

Tsui attempts to narrate part of this confusion in her discussion of how race and ethnicity are so easily conflated. At one point in the op-ed, she states, "So what's my problem with Asian salad? It's not the salad itself, though it's not my favorite. It's the words—which, I think, matter. In many ways, the broad, generic terminology used to refer to an entire continent is the heart of it." Here, she explicitly calls out common US conceptions of Asian Americans as monolithic, seemingly upset with the lack of attention to ethnicity among broader discussions of race.[38] In response to her concern for ethnic multiplicity, many of the commentators explicitly narrate their own experiences with European ethnic specificity as a model of how focusing on cultural details leads to division and strife. For example, Hugh Jones elucidates a range of stereotypical Italian cultural touchstones as a way of demonstrating his proclaimed Italian identity in order to mock the supposed emphasis on authenticity. He finishes his statement by directly calling out one of Tsui's sentences; at one point, she states, "When I see an Oriental Chop Chop or a Secret Asian Man, I feel . . . weary." In response, Hugh Jones details his ethnic background and attempts to compare it with her discussion.

---

37. Nakayama and Krizek, "Whiteness: A Strategic Rhetoric," 300. See also Bond, "Whitewashing Ancient Statues."

38. Catherine Prendergast reminds us that the director of *Crash*, Paul Haggis, saw nothing wrong with "cast[ing] two Korean people and then decid[ing] to call them Chinamen, because that's what we do in America. [. . .] We sort of lump all groups together" ("Asians," 347).

I am a third-generation Italian-American (Hugh Jones is not my real name, I
don't wanting anyone writing and reading in NYT remarks sections knowing
who I really am) and every time I see a drawing of that buffoonish, cartoon-
ish, overweight guy with the mustache and the kerchief around his neck who
is the logo for countless pizza shops, Italian restaurants, and prepared foods,
I become enraged. Ms. Tsui, I hope you are not ordering items in an "Italian" restaurant that could possibly be run by Poles or Irish people, because
that would be an affront to me personally. The only ones making anything
"Italian" should be guys like me.

Ditto shows like The Sopranos, movies like Good Fellas—makes me feel
like people making those movies and shows are saying to me personally "you
are a gun-toting, meatball-eating crook."

So please, Ms. Tsui, I'll stop eating Asian salad if you stop eating all that
"Italian" stuff that was not personally made by one of my relatives in Italy.
Anything less makes me . . . weary.

Instead of taking up Tsui's point about the intersection of language and perception of other ethnicities, this commentator instead decides to spoof Tsui's
performance of emotional weariness through a reduction of Italian culture
to pizza shops and blockbuster movies. The sarcasm operates as a distorted
mirror of Tsui's argument and intentions, placing her in a defensive position
where she must account for her excesses of sensitivity that renders her too
focused on ethnicity. For example, the moment where he "become[s] enraged"
is meant as a clear moment of hyperbole (one does not typically become
enraged upon seeing a cartoon character) that operates as judgment that her
pathos is too excessive for the subject. By focusing this mock offense on body
image and performing a thick-skinned machoness, he reduces the issue into
one of personal insecurity about one's physical appearance. Tsui is only bothered by such trivialities as ethnic stereotypes because of personal insecurities.
Thus, the commentator, and those who agree with him, are not only more
culturally harmonious but also more secure in their own skin. In following
up with the comment that "the only ones making anything 'Italian' should
be guys like me," the commentator is also attributing motivations of deprivation and cultural policing to Tsui. The enthymeme running in the background
implies that those who become so overly sensitive about naming conventions
for food are equally concerned with policing authenticity.

These contradictory attempts to both use and disavow ethnic identity is
reminiscent of what Christa Olson describes as the white-mestizos' strategic
leveraging of indigenous identity in Banõs, Ecuador. She argues they were
able to rhetorically perform as "Indians" because of "a slippage between what

we might call 'real' indigeneity and the nexus of circumstances and attributes that signal indigeneity. Or, to appropriate Robert Berkhofer's terms, in order to understand the workings of the embodiable topos, we must acknowledge the distinction between 'real' indigenous people and the 'Indian' as a colonial invention."[39] The white-mestizos drew on a range of available images and descriptions of indigenous peoples that held certain sympathetic tropes and then wielded them in various permutations to claim some of that sympathetic identity for themselves. In the *New York Times* comments, there is a similar slippage between claiming an identity that is more aligned with whiteness and references to experiences that signal significant contact with the Other as a means of gaining progressive social capital. Although these commentators understand that they might be perceived by outsiders as white, they purposefully forward their store of ethnic knowledge as a progressive point for their own ethos. The fact that the commentators are also part of a group portrayed via humorous visual signifiers and cultural stereotypes on film is presented as an equivocating gesture, enabling them to perform a more enlightened ethos that is not offended by such trivial concerns.

PERFORMING THE "RIGHT" SORT OF ASIAN

Alongside the negative comments from those who claim a non-Asian identity, there are also a number of commentators who explicitly claim some form of Asianness as evidence against Tsui and her argument. Regardless of the commentators' intentions, the bulk effect of these comments is a recentering of the "model minority" as the normative identity for Asian Americans through disidentification with Tsui's provocation. In order to fit into this fictitious category, the minority is expected to self-discipline via "self-styling techniques that include the denial and displacement of their paradoxical position in relation to narratives of citizenship and belonging" in order to achieve a level of "honorary whiteness."[40] The popular myths of the treacherous Asian seductress and the real-life examples of individuals like Tokyo Rose and Hanoi Hannah mean that "Asian American women must perform a radicalized and gendered display of national fidelity to make up for what is considered their predisposition to treachery and betrayal."[41] The expectation that females are overly emotional is doubled within Asian embodiment. In reading Tsui's approach to writing, one can see her own awareness of this delicate negotiation between

39. Olson, "Performing Embodiable Topoi," 304–5.
40. Yoon, "Learning Asian American Affect," 300.
41. Yoon, "Learning Asian American Affect," 301.

model and harpy when she states, "The casual racism of the Asian salad stems from the idea of the exotic—who is and isn't American is caught up wholesale in its creation. This use of 'Oriental' and 'Asian' is rooted in the wide-ranging, 'all look same' stereotypes of Asian culture that most people don't really perceive as being racist. It creates a kind of blind spot."[42] For Tsui, the salad names are where "that blind spot reveals itself," although she does not go so far as to name who created this gap in the racial imaginary. She hedges further— "casual racism," "don't really perceive," and "kind of blind spot"—so as to create a more neutral emotional tone. To be angry would to be unaware of all the "advantages" she receives as a member of the model minority. Even with these hedges, she is still accused of writing a "self-serving diatribe" (Michael Devine, April 28, 2017) and of being a "special cultural snowflake" (Honeybee, April 27, 2017). These responses demonstrate the double bind that Tsui is in as a visibly Asian American subject. As Ngai points out, "Emotional qualities seem especially prone to sliding into corporeal qualities where the [racialized] subject is concerned, reinforcing the notion of race as a truth located, quite naturally, in the always obvious, highly visible body."[43] To perform emotion is to risk aligning with preexisting imaginings of the too-sensitive or excitable body that exemplifies the worst qualities of one's race.

With this in mind, the commentators that claim Asianness as a counter to Tsui are performing a claim to whiteness, or at least proximity to it, that adheres more to the safe realm of the model minority. Asian Americans are expected to perform what Tina Chen calls "imposture" as one's main mode of identity. If to be Asian in America is to always be a possible threat of contagion or violence, to occupy an identity that "has, from its earliest moments in U.S. legal and social history, been constituted as an oxymoron," then to be Asian American is always a process of impersonating a racial coherency that has been decided elsewhere.[44] We see the full expression of these contradictory model minority expectations from commentators who explicitly claim an Asian or Asian American identity in order to separate themselves from Tsui's position.

> Please get a life. I'm very proud of my chinese [sic] heritage but find it childish to get upset by these trivialities. (luis, April 27, 2017)

---

42. Tsui's use of an ableist metaphor demonstrates the need for continued conversations about intersectionality.

43. Ngai, *Ugly Feelings*, 95.

44. T. Chen, *Double Agency*, 19.

Oh please. I am Asian and will eat an Asian salad from Panera Bread without any angst. Get over it. Must be nice to have so much time on your hands! (Leslie T, April 27, 2017)

OMG . . . you have nothing better to write about. Much ado about nothing. Let's solve some real world problems instead of more of this identity politics now caught up in salad. (FYI—I am proud Chinese-American, 3rd generation immigrant). (GS, April 28, 2017)

I'm Chinese American. Love Asian salad even though I appreciate my authentic Chinese food very much. Never thought Asian salad is racism. Love that it's ubiquitous. This person to me is looking for a problem when there really isn't. I think it stems from her actually not liking Asian salad. (Lana, April 27, 2017)

If there is soy or sesame in the dressing or perhaps a bit of miso—then it's Asian! I'm happy to see that these flavors are beloved by many. Don't look for insults where none is intended! BTW, I'm Korean. (HopBella, April 27, 2017)

This claiming of racial/ethnic identity in direct opposition to not just Tsui's argument but also her emotional gestalt is an assimilative rhetorical move, aimed at reducing the distance between Asian American and American by proclaiming an ideological perspective that attempts to forestall accusations of non-national allegiances—the "American" is the most important part of "Asian American." In this framework, the mentions of more specific ethnic allegiances, such as "BTW I'm Korean," serve not to disrupt understandings of Asians as the model minority but rather to reaffirm belief in the post-racial promise of a homogenized Asian interchangeability.

What is important to recognize is that the quick move to "I am X Asian, but I feel Tsui is wrong" only resonates if the preexisting expectation is that Asians all think and act in lockstep. It is the performed awareness of perceived racial/ethnic similarities between themselves and Tsui, the violation of expected racial solidarity, that gives this sort of rhetorical move its weight. The purported novelty of an Asian American claiming to go against most of their racial category builds their individual ethos as fair-minded even as it relies on outdated notions of an Asian community that is unified in outlook and behavior. Barbara Warnick points out how factual and value-based knowledge intermingle in topical arguing: To be effective, "the rhetor must also know the values, presumptions, predispositions, and expectations of the audience, and he must locate both his starting points (special topics) and forms of inference (common topics) with these in mind."[45] Here, there is a tacitly assumed white audience to be persuaded, and the Asian commentators make identity-based attributions that align with the multicultural emphasis on collecting types of food/people so often valued in white-dominant spheres.

Therefore, telling Tsui to not "look for insults" and to not be so "childish" as to be upset by such "trivialities" is not just a policing of Tsui's behavior but also a demonstration of the expected Asian American traits of maturity, seriousness, and equanimity that Tsui obviously lacks. Tsui is not performing the "cultural labor exacted of Asian American women" that works to "discipline dominant subjects to maintain the polite and cheerful veneer that supports the American Dream ideology."[46] The Asian commentators are marking her as a body that can and should be questioned for its departure from normativity as it moves through dominant spaces. In this case, performing a white or white-adjacent identity means to inhabit a body that is the right level of sensitive. Such a body is not overemotional but tastefully so, able to distinguish and appreciate a diversity of ethnic cuisines.

This particular understanding of diversity is especially clear in a comment by DK.

> As an "actual" Asian-American, I'm not offended. However, you are not qualified to voice my feelings nor are you qualified to judge what a "white audience" thinks.
>
> Also, why generalize the "white audience"? What about Blacks, Latinos, Native Americans, etc., etc.?
>
> I am so sick of these articles which take offense to every perceived slight. Sure, racism still exists but can we take a break and celebrate how far we've all come together in the relatively past few years? (April 29, 2017)

Here, the commentator distances themselves from Tsui by recentering the idea of "actual" Asian Americans around multicultural unity by pointing to "how far we've all come together," but the framing in terms of a collaborative journey hints at the fear of loss that is a core part of the model minority narrative. The "factioning, fractioning, and fractilizing of identity is a prime activity of societies of control, whereby subjects (the ethnic, the homonormative) orient themselves as subjects through their disassociation or disidentification from others disenfranchised in similar ways in favor of consolidation with axes of privilege."[47] Rather than reject the model minority category, this and

---

45. Warnick, "Two Systems of Invention," 108.
46. Yoon, "Learning Asian American Affect," 296.
47. Puar, *Terrorist Assemblages*, 28.

similar comments forward a version of the world in which the racial equilibrium should not disturbed because to do so risks one's place in the queue for social privilege.

These comments in particular demonstrate the rhetorical burden on Asian speakers and writers who attempt to challenge racial hierarchies. For those who must speak from within the expectations of the model minority stereotype, there is a sense of "feeling torn between a hegemonic polarity that demands that allegiance must always be rendered to a singularly defined identity."[48] We see how these commentators, more than just presenting a united front against Tsui, are pairing the topos of sensitivity with an explicit racial ethos in order to claim an Asian identity that is less threatening, more American, than what they perceive Tsui as performing. Since to be Asian in the American context is to be overtly marked upon sight, this state of being means having to constantly perform an ethos that is model enough as judged by the majority, which often means ignoring, or in this case, replicating microaggressions found in dominant discourses. In psychological studies, microaggressions related to race often "negate the significance of identity in the lives of marginalized individuals" as an operation of gaslighting, of getting the individual to believe that they are being "too sensitive."[49] Throughout the responses from those who identity from within a particular Asian group, drawing on microinvalidation is a way of distancing the writer from the faceless mass of stereotypical Asians: For example, the comment of "You have nothing better to write about" trivializes not only Tsui's argument but also her intellectual scope, a rhetorical move that automatically places her outside of the model minority position and, therefore, outside of the acceptable bounds of Asian American identity.

CONCLUSIONS

Ignoring microaggressive patterns in favor of pat multicultural decorum is part of a broader set of enduring attitudes toward Asians and their place in America. While #StopAsianHate arose in response to the unignorable rise in violence against Asian Americans during President Trump's term in office and the spread of COVID, the attacks and hateful incidents continued under President Biden. After the murder of eight people, six of whom were Asian women,

---

48. Mannur, *Culinary Fictions*, 178.

49. Ong et al., "Racial Microaggressions," 189. See also O'Keefe et al., "Seemingly Harmless Racial Communications" for research on how microaggressions can lead to harmful mental changes, such as increased susceptibility to depression and suicidal ideation.

at a health spa in Atlanta, Georgia, in March 2021, a police captain stated at a news conference that the crime happened not because of racist misogyny but because the shooter was having a "really bad day." As the Margaret Cho quote used at the beginning of this chapter indicates, the range of allowable public emotion, and thus rhetorical options, is inseparable from assumptions about who is expected to have feelings about race. The backlash to Tsui's argument, grounded in arguments about emotional decorum, demonstrates how these expectations of the passive, feminine Asian figure that supports post-racial harmony can be used to gloss over everyday attitudes that are most visible in times of overt violence but that nonetheless endure in even more ostensibly peaceful times. The expectation of decorum is a tool of whiteness that is often used to elide the real issues at hand, superseding vulnerable voices in favor of polished, status quo statements. In the case of Tsui and the outsized response to her relatively trivial point about salad names, we see how acting outside of the emotional norms attached to the identity stereotype of "model minority" results in a variety of interconnected rhetorical moves all aimed at maintaining the racial status quo.

In considering how the topoi of sensitivity and ethnic authenticity can be used together to rhetorically reject substantial engagement with racial hierarchies, it also becomes clearer how the linkage of Asianness and food is part of a broader rhetorical orientation toward race that figures consumption as a unidirectional extraction of cultural capital from the politicized figure of the Other. The imagined space of these interactions with difference is one in which ethnicity, especially in relation to food, is a salable curiosity within a free marketplace, unbound by more complicated racial histories. The broader, more notable conflicts between racial groups are muted, which means that it becomes possible to rhetorically frame difference as a mostly trivial aspect that can and should be overcome in favor of allegiance to the American melting pot ideal. The exchange of cultural knowledge is a matter of individual willingness to share as a move toward intercultural engagement, which leaves those who wish to engage with race and ethnicity in ways other than capitalistic exchange without many rhetorical options. Tsui's argument is misaligned with a gut orientation where Asian Americans are expected to perform for a white-minded audience both in terms of taste (either aesthetic or flavor-related) and emotion. Rhetoricians should watch for this sort of argumentative move, where the rejection of types of emotional expression is predicated on an assumed baseline for emotional behavior that diminishes and silences outliers.

There are spaces to reject anticipated silencing and instead craft the voicing of resistance and alternative narratives. In response to the vitriolic criticism of Tsui, the online magazine *Civil Eats* ran an article where they interviewed Tsui and several other food writers on how they have handled such public backlash to their work.[50] Among many of the responses from writers such as Stephen Satterfield, Tsui, and Tunde Wey, the common thread was the need for more attention to voices from writers of color and the setting up of support systems for those already writing, along with holding people accountable for willful misreadings and attacks. Stephen Satterfield puts it this way: "Abolishing racial inequity endures as the work of the privileged, and so intrinsically needs to [be] loudly shouted down not by the writers who are the target of the racism, but by 'everyone else.' For the rest of 'us,' the work continues. Keep writing." Satterfield's words, although addressed to the community of food writers and activists, resonate with rhetorical work that seeks to not just uncover latent racism in public discourses but develop new networks of support and mentorship. In addition to the legitimacy of anger as a response to racist vitriol, the "shouting down" of people we see abusing others, there is also a need for the creation of spaces that enable writers themselves to express the full range of their emotions that relate to the interconnection of race, food, and embodiment. In order to activate new forms of discourse that enable more voices to be heard and, thus, more lives to be understood, work is needed to provide channels for unabridged expression that work to dismantle racist emotional norms.

---

50. Tsui et al., "Why We Can't Talk about Race."

CONCLUSION

Unmooring Habits of Taste

> As a Chinese immigrant, my body is seen as a fruiting body in a
> sinister yellow fungal network, grown too fast and too power-
> ful, primed to release spores of disease across the world.
>
> —Zoe Yang, "As Coronavirus Panic Spreads"

It is difficult to speak about race and the associated axes of gender, sexuality, class, and so on without referencing *violence against* in some form. Symbolic violence at the macro or micro level. Physical violence enacted via top-down systemic oppression or sidewalk encounters that turn ugly. Abrasive, threatening language. The role of the rhetorical critic is, in part, to point to how the one violent encounter emerges from constitutive rhetorical practices that make hierarchies of brutality seem normal. I see this book as aligning with such critical impulses even as I focus on how the complexity of racial interrelations and associated inequities is not just found in violent extremes but also rooted in the everyday mundane of consumption.

In *Inscrutable Eating*, I have explored how the stories we tell about people and their appetites are inextricable from tacit assumptions about race, gender, and sexuality. Or, proclivities of the mouth are assumed to signal proclivities of other organs. As such, the stories we tell about foods and eating are never neutral but bear undertones of moral judgment, assumptions about citizenship and belonging, and expectations for proximity and intimacy among bodies. These assumptions become especially evident when analyzing discourses related to Asian food and eaters within the US; the presumed foreignness of the Asian body means that consumption of Asian foods, however pleasurable, is always a potential gateway into outsider contamination.

I have theorized the concept of gut orientations in order to better understand how we are drawn to certain constellations of bodies and objects over others based on presumed habits of consumption. In so doing, it becomes clear how the same flows of affective and rhetorical force that render *proximity to* as a key part of social hierarchies are intertwined with axes of race, gender, sexuality, and class. Orientations of bodies and gazes are not neutral but are rooted in broader ecologies of judgment about what is disgusting or threatening, who disgusts or threatens. On its own, the use of the term "orientation" as a guiding metaphor might lend itself to understanding this sort of rhetorical work as a mere shift in perspective, a re-placing of the body in a different position with different eyelines and atmospheres. What I have attempted to signal with my choice of the additional term "gut" is how the process of reorienting is itself never neutral but continually underpinned by tacit, affectively powerful accumulations of desire and repulsion. Resetting orientations toward objects and others is a complex resetting of deeply felt boundaries. The sort of reorientation that is necessary to rewrite understandings of appropriate interrelations between racialized bodies and their products (words, foods, smells, etc.) is sometimes not even seen as an option through the mists of repugnance. Part of understanding rhetorical possibilities on a gut level means understanding what happens when empathy curdles.

The four examples of gut orientations discussed in this book show how the judgment of appropriate distance from racialized Others, whether related to miscegenation, cohabitation, or citizenship, is inextricable from judgments of appropriate expressions of eating, sex, and emotion. In labeling Chinese immigrants as rats and rat eaters, anti-Asian advocates in the 1800s were able to encourage more distance between races as a prophylactic measure, a thread that emerged again in the chaos of the COVID-19 pandemic and derogatory narratives about eating bats. Even beyond overt discrimination, these embedded ideas of Asianness as subtly contaminating reproduce fixed distances among racialized bodies as normal at best, but these topoi can also provide validation for overt violence against Asian bodies. As seen in the discourse on MSG and wellness, those with control over the framing of food products can create conditions for racist distancing all while proclaiming a nonracist stance through a focus on unclean or otherwise undesirable foods. Similarly, the rapidity with which an emotional Asian is cast as an overemotional Asian, a "too sensitive" rhetor, is part of this overarching understanding of a flawed Asian embodiment that needs to quietly submit to racial hierarchies as the price for continued membership in US society. Throughout these examples, the underlying assumption is that a violation of consumption is linked to an inherently flawed performance of race, gender, sexuality, and/or class.

In exploring how the rhetorical process of racialization occurs in discourses on and practices around food, it is impossible to ignore how understandings of race are deeply embedded within embodiments on a quick-twitch level of physiological response. Our understanding of race is the totality of discourses, affects, bodily habits, and movements that collectively inform our sensemaking of other people and our relation to them. The gut is a prime place for the enactment of this tacit sensual understanding of the organization of the world, as the gut is where it is acceptable to forefront pathic heuristics. Gut reactions are habitual enactions of race that fade into the background as the rightness of the everyday. This sense of rightness is embedded within one's bodily history in how "our bodies are trained to navigate the world from stores of embodied, affective attachments to certain affiliations or investments, attachments that make some rhetorical paths more or less appealing than others."[1] These habitual ways of engaging with the world, due to environments and allegiances, underpin how we are able to engage with specific factors like race, class, and gender. In other words, attitudes toward race are not absent when they are not voiced. Rather, these attitudes emerge in gut orientations that are felt in terms of comfort or discomfort that come into focus around certain physicalities, objects, and actions.

The foods and eaters that fall into the category of the ordinary abject are necessary for the maintenance of normative limits around performances of race, gender, sexuality, and class. Lisa Flores argues that the affective circulations of "hope and threat" are the building blocks for racialization of the Mexican migrant as a willing source of disposable labor in opposition to the self-actualized, white American citizen.[2] I argue that a similarly illogical framework of Asianness as simultaneously alluring and repulsive is channeled through the object of food and action of eating, setting expectations for Asianness as expected to dance between these two poles of "yellow peril" and "model minority" as needed for the non-Asian norm to maintain its superiority. Exceeding these preset categories is not a lack of imagination on the part of the non-Asian interlocutor but rather a failure of the Asian body to meet anticipated probabilities. Corporeal ambivalence is not allowed in the normative, interrelational limits of such a metric.

This contradiction is baked into dominant forms of racial recognition, which means that macro, structural inequities are but one element that needs to be addressed in the quest for full social equality. Because large issues like economic disparities are made possible through a range of affective nudges,

---

1. LeMesurier, "Somatic Metaphors," 364.
2. Flores, *Deportable and Disposable*, 150.

manifest in daily actions or inactions, that maintain norms for proximity between the eater and the repelled, addressing social injustice requires attending to the microaggressive gut. For example, the "bamboo ceiling" enables us to see inequity in hiring at top positions in the corporate world, but the metaphor's emphasis on upward financial movement as an automatic positive cannot fully encompass the practices, rhetorical and otherwise, that inform inclusion and exclusion. We need to consider other metaphors for racial inequities and biases besides those that rely on the vertical, especially as focusing on economic rankings might actually reinforce the inequities we are trying to ameliorate, just along different axes. In approaching this problem via the concept of gut orientation, we can better see how it is not just the presence of one or even multiple bodies at "the top" that indicate if a society has a race problem. Rather, it is the patterned layers of distances and proximities, constellations that become fixed as presumed veridicalities, that need to be untangled rather than just rearranged. The unquestioned status of everyday emotion-object and emotion-subject pathways is part of a broader rhetorical orientation toward the world at large where one centers oneself by measuring the distance from Others via the levels of fear/disgust and comfort/desire with food and consumption.

The recurrence and easy acceptance of the trope of Asians as bodies with distorted appetites supports the ongoing understanding of Asians as those from away, still loyal to homelands that they would slot into neatly should they return, as opposed to the slightly jagged fit in their American residences. Such an understanding, although gentler than previous eras' emphasis on overt eradication or displacement, is nonetheless predicated on maintaining (at the least) distance between groups of bodies. The lack of national attention to discrimination and violence against Asian Americans prior to 2020 is not solely a matter of activist energy or effort but rather is part of the dominant orientation that sees Asianness as more invested in other geographies, as evidenced by spicy and strange palates. It took the global crisis of a pandemic to recognize acts of anti-Asian hatred that are but the continuation of longstanding biases and omission of consideration in race-related conversations.

Often, eating an Other's food is held up as a triumph for intercultural relations, yet the case studies in this book demonstrate how the centering of the sensual pleasure of eating does not automatically disrupt the accompanying assumed fears and titillations that keep that Asian food outside of the mainstream. As bell hooks states, "Acknowledging ways the desire for pleasure, and that includes erotic longings, informs our politics, our understanding of difference, we may know better how desire disrupts, subverts, and makes resistance possible. We cannot, however, accept these new images uncritically."[3] To pin hopes on cultural food as a racial equalizer too easily elides the commodification of race in a globally interconnected world and the forms of bodily inherency that are used to make positive claims about these Othered bodies; the underlying warrants that render food, culture, and bodies synedochical can be rhetorically leveraged against these bodies in discourses of exclusion and xenophobia. Gut orientations that support such assumptions can be pressed into service "over time to protect whiteness and its beneficiaries" through framing historical patterns of racial violence and discrimination as isolated events that are long behind us, rather than the logical end of ongoing misrepresentations.[4] What this means is that positive narratives of racial identification might still be rooted in an overhomogenizing gut orientation that demands adherence to dominant stereotypes by patrolling the feelings or sensations these bodies evoke.

The specificity of these beliefs about racialized embodiment explains how narratives of deviance or other nonnormative behavior endure even as language becomes more inclusive. Especially in rhetoric, there is a need for more explicit considerations of how judgments about bodily legitimacy, and thus ethos and agency, are inseparable from supposedly personal matters of taste. I focus here on discourses related to food and consumption, but the broader exigency is understanding how histories and biases are rendered into supposed inherencies of the flesh that remain unquestioned in the background. These suasions emerge in beliefs about behavior, but they are indebted to categorical ways of thinking about bodies and identity, about tribes that think and eat like you. The task for critical rhetorical scholars, alongside continuing to demystify bad arguments and elevate good ones, is to practice attending to the role of the body in these debates with recognition of where the visceral takes primacy in the formation of rhetorical influence.

Beyond the realm of eating, one way to apply gut orientations is in finegrained analyses of which affects are at work in combination with which arguments. Affect, as temporarily coalesced bundles of feelings and sensations, bears traces of previous narratives and ideologies. The original rhetorical work that must be done to make certain forms of affect feel legitimate remains even after events or situations are repurposed. Race, as a material process of reimpressing bodies into feeling ease with certain ways of navigating others, and vice versa, is a collection of enduring affective impressions and prior rhetori-

---

3. hooks, "Eating the Other," 39.
4. Houdek, "Racial Sedimentation," 281.

cal work. In other words, one must attend to the associated traces of affect in the taking up and incorporation of rhetorics. As is evident in the case of Asian food and eaters, the broad mesh of affect and materials that structure incentives for inhabiting one's body in alignment with social norms also supports thinking of Asianness as separate from such norms. Rhetorical methodologies need to account for more fully embodied awareness and stratagems that will help unpack the traces of overtly harmful ideologies in the seemingly personal moments of second glances or recoils. Centering the gut in rhetorical analysis requires looking for how rhetoric that happens in the everyday accumulates into a leaning *away from*. It is this accumulation, this resulting gut orientation, that alters what pathways we see as possible, for ourselves and others. These orientations might be obvious in explicit discourses of hatred and disgust, but they might also remain in the silences that occur because agreement is too obvious to be said aloud.

More concretely, thinking with the gut means looking for patterns of discourse and behavior that avow leaning into or away from certain bodies as a preferred stance. As stated previously, I am influenced by Michael McGee's guiding metaphor of rhetorical fragments, but I am particularly interested in how fragments on seemingly unrelated subjects add up to an unquestioned sense of bodily limits. Descriptions of specific bodies are a good place to start. How is the body in question positioned, and how does that positioning itself project a normative, external viewer? And at what distance is that viewer assumed to stand? Whether in the case of rat, bat, or MSG eaters, it is not just that such bodies are described in terms of primitivity or animality but that they are presented as the convex to the upright, non-bat-eating reader. Beliefs about race, rurality, national identity, and cleanliness jostle and overlap in their attribution to this one person. In analyzing how bodies are described, positioned in relation to other bodies, amplified or denigrated, ascribed to certain spatiotemporal orders over others, and so on, we better understand the level of existing audience receptivity for such a depiction and more clearly see which discriminatory affects need to be dismantled. The further step needed is an explicit unpacking of the underlying warrants of sensation and emotion that contribute to the building of such a body. As seen in the discussion of Asian food by wellness influencers, these dishes are described in positive terms of tastiness and craving, but these positive attributions are counterbalanced by beliefs that Asian food naturally produces certain sensations that signal future physical harm. The personal reaction encapsulates macro-level attitudes and moral judgments in habituations, and as such offers insight into how certain rhetorical messages around identity are maintained.

My hope in centering the object of food and actions of eating as racialized is to highlight how everyday matters of taste and desire are not separate from the ideological work of critical rhetoric. Views we might disavow as harmful when written or spoken might still operate when we choose what to leave off our plates. I speak here, of course, not just of matters of purchasing and consumption, although supporting underrepresented makers is important in a capitalist society. Rather, I ask us to consider what sensations we choose to listen to and center, which "gut feelings" we accept as truths and which affective lineages are scrutinized, in order to clarify how past euphorias and eureka moments exert guiding force on the bodies we find more comfortable, most fitting, and most legitimate. Such deep attention is necessary for future rhetorical work on the deep embeddedness of racial bias as it operates in both direct exhortations and the quiet absence of dissent.

APPENDIX

New York Times Comments on "Asian Salad"

In order to code comments,[1] I started with an in vivo approach, looking for "names that are the exact words used by participants" in order to identify themes that were triggered by Tsui's own rhetorical strategies within the article.[2] What were the flash points that people were responding to, and what rhetorical structures were people using to respond to those points? This resulted in eighteen original codes that were focused on explicit mentions or discussions within the comments (see below). Some of these codes were not centered on a particular word or phrase but on a repeated explicit pattern of rhetorical approach, as in code 5. Many of the comments contained multiple codes. Once I coded all the comments, I looked first to see the ratio of the codes used to support or oppose Tsui's argument; the comments were overwhelmingly in opposition. Then, I considered what themes and patterns crossed and linked together different codes. For example, if a comment contained codes 2, 6, and 14, was there a thematic in that comment's argument that could be found in a comment with a different permutation of codes? Overwhelmingly, the themes that tended to cross and link codes together was the issue of authenticity as

---

1. Since 2007, the *New York Times* has allowed comments on the majority of its news articles, and the comments are moderated to remove extremely partisan, offensive, or completely irrelevant posts. Tsui's article received 644 comments and replies. When edited for repeat or nonsensical comments, the corpus stands at 603 comments and replies.

2. Creswell, *Qualitative Inquiry*, 185.

it relates to food and culture and the appropriate level of sensitivity to racial slight. As most of the comments were negatively inclined toward Tsui and/or her argument, these topoi of authenticity and sensitivity became pivot points where the commentators could criticize Tsui's take and then demonstrate their own commitment to a weak idea of difference as defined by their own connections with race and ethnicity.

Another prominent thread in the responses to Tsui was the overt presence of hyperbole and sarcasm, which I grouped together in code 5. Although these comments did not necessarily directly address Tsui's race, there is a prominent emphasis on exploding the discourse around race so as to render it null, often by offering extreme examples of the commentator's own presumed ethnic identity markers. It does this by rendering the object of race as not merely trivial but as a superfluous prop for humor. Once the reader has "got the joke," the point of reading or thinking further dissipates. As with the other responses, these ranged the gamut from short, snarky comments ("This opinion piece would have worked better in the Onion") to longer diatribes against political correctness. Similar to the racial/ethnic ethos descriptions in code 10, there are several extended examples that focus on mocking Tsui's sensitivity.

1. "Why Trump won"—also sometimes extended to a more general negative comment about the Republican party
2. "I am X race or ethnicity"
3. "I have friends/family who are X race or ethnicity"
4. "PC"/"snowflakes"
5. Hyperbolic riffing on what else to be offended by / sarcasm
6. References to Jewish identity
7. Listing of other food examples, either to support or negate Tsui's point, for example, "Belgian Waffles"
8. A discussion of a historical example or nuance, for example, the "actual" or "official" origin of a certain dish
9. Exasperation / a desire to discuss more "serious" issues
10. The author as being "too sensitive"
11. Reference to person of note, for example, chef David Chang
12. Liberal/democrat
13. Calling on Tsui and others for using the term "white" hypocritically
14. Attribution of any racist or racialized meaning to corporate greed/disinterest
15. Pointing out of an example from an Asian country that Tsui did not cite

16. Explicit calls for more focus on one's American identity / more nationalist unity

17. Examples from one's own world travels of potentially fraught or offensive incidents

18. Criticism of the food itself, for example, "All chain food is bad quality."

BIBLIOGRAPHY

Ahmad, Diana L. "Opium Smoking, Anti-Chinese Attitudes, and the American Medical Community, 1850–1890." *American Nineteenth Century History* 1, no. 2 (2000): 53–68.

Ahmed, Sara. *The Cultural Politics of Emotion.* Edinburgh: Edinburgh University Press, 2014.

———. "Orientations: Toward a Queer Phenomenology." *GLQ: A Journal of Lesbian and Gay Studies* 12, no. 4 (2006): 543–74.

———. *Queer Phenomenology: Orientations, Objects, Others.* Durham: Duke University Press, 2006.

———. "Racialized Bodies." In *Real Bodies: A Sociological Introduction,* edited by Mary Evans and Ellie Lee, 46–63. New York: Palgrave, 2002.

Ajinomoto. "#RedefineCRS." knowmsg.com. https://www.knowmsg.com/chinese-restaurant-syndrome/.

Alvarez, Steven. "Some More on Taco USA, History, and Instagram." *Taco Literacy: Writing Transnational Mexican Foodways* (blog), February 6, 2018. https://tacoliteracy.com/2018/02/06/828/.

Anzaldúa, Gloria. *Borderlands / La Frontera: The New Mestiza.* San Francisco: Aunt Lute Books, 1987.

Bailey, Cathryn. "We Are What We Eat: Feminist Vegetarianism and the Reproduction of Racial Identity." *Hypatia* 22, no. 2 (2007): 39–59.

Bain, David Haward. *Empire Express: Building the First Transcontinental Railroad.* New York: Viking, 1999.

Bargh, John A., and Katelyn Y. A. McKenna. "The Internet and Social Life." *Annual Review of Psychology* 55, no. 1 (2004): 573–90.

Bekiempis, Victoria. "R. Kelly's Lawyer Tries to Discredit Alleged Victim with . . . Chinese Food." *Vulture,* September 9, 2021. https://www.vulture.com/2021/09/r-kelly-trial-lawyer-victim-chinese-food-msg.html.

"Better Than Takeout: Four Chinese Food Recipes to Make at Home." *Goop.* Accessed May 18, 2022. https://goop.com/food/recipes/better-than-takeout-four-chinese-food-recipes-anyone-can-make-at-home/.

Bhabha, Homi K. *The Location of Culture.* New York: Routledge, 2004.

Biltekoff, Charlotte. *Eating Right in America: The Cultural Politics of Food and Health.* Durham, NC: Duke University Press, 2013.

Bond, Sarah. "Whitewashing Ancient Statues: Whiteness, Racism, and Color in the Ancient World." *Forbes,* April 27, 2017. https://www.forbes.com/sites/drsarahbond/2017/04/27/whitewashing-ancient-statues-whiteness-racism-and-color-in-the-ancient-world/.

Bonilla-Silva, Eduardo, Carla Goar, and David G. Embrick. "When Whites Flock Together: The Social Psychology of White Habitus." *Critical Sociology* 32, no. 2–3 (2006): 229–53.

Bow, Leslie. *Partly Colored: Asian Americans and Racial Anomaly in the Segregated South.* New York: New York University Press, 2010.

———. "Racist Cute: Caricature, Kawaii-Style, and the Asian Thing." *American Quarterly* 71, no. 1 (2019): 29–58.

———. *Racist Love: Asian Abstraction and the Pleasures of Fantasy.* Durham, NC: Duke University Press, 2022.

Bright, Rachel K. "Migration, Masculinity, and Mastering the Queue: A Case of Chinese Scalping." *Journal of World History* 28, no. 3/4 (2017): 551–86.

Brock, André. "'Who Do You Think You Are?': Race, Representation, and Cultural Rhetorics in Online Spaces." *Poroi* 6, no. 1 (2009): 15–35.

Bubb, Claire. "The Physiology of Phantasmata in Aristotle: Between Sensation and Digestion." *Apeiron* 52, no. 3 (2019): 273–315.

Bui, Long. "Asian Roboticism: Connecting Mechanized Labor to the Automation of Work." *Perspectives on Global Development and Technology* 19 (2020): 110–26.

Burke, Kenneth. *A Rhetoric of Motives.* Berkeley: University of California Press, 1969.

Butler, Judith. *Bodies That Matter: On the Discursive Limits of Sex.* London: Routledge, 2011.

Campbell, Charlie, and Alice Park. "Inside the Global Quest to Trace the Origins of COVID-19 and Predict Where It Will Go Next." *Time,* July 23, 2020. https://time.com/5870481/coronavirus-origins/.

Campeau, Kari L. "Vaccine Barriers, Vaccine Refusals: Situated Vaccine Decision-Making in the Wake of the 2017 Minnesota Measles Outbreak." *Rhetoric of Health & Medicine* 2, no. 2 (2019): 176–207.

Cannato, Vincent J. "How America Became Italian." *Washington Post,* Oct. 15, 2015. http://wapo.st/1LDUqxQ?tid=ss_tw.

Chang, Gordon H. "The Chinese and the Stanfords: Nineteenth-Century America's Fraught Relationship with the China Men." In *The Chinese and the Iron Road: Building the Transcontinental Railroad,* edited by Gordon H. Chang and Shelly F. Fishkin, 346–64. Stanford, CA: Stanford University Press, 2019.

Chang, Gordon H., and Shelly F. Fishkin. Introduction to *The Chinese and the Iron Road: Building the Transcontinental Railroad,* 1–26. Edited by Gordon H. Chang and Shelly F. Fishkin. Stanford, CA: Stanford University Press, 2019.

Chaput, Catherine. "The Body as a Site of Material-Symbolic Struggle: Toward a Marxist New Materialism." *Philosophy & Rhetoric* 53, no. 1 (2020): 89–103.

Chávez, Karma R. "The Body: An Abstract and Actual Rhetorical Concept." *Rhetoric Society Quarterly* 48, no. 3 (May 2018): 242–50. Accessed June 21, 2021. https://doi.org/10.1080/0277 3945.2018.1454182.

———. *Queer Migration Politics: Activist Rhetoric and Coalitional Possibilities.* Urbana: University of Illinois Press, 2013.

Chen, Mel Y. "Agitation." *The South Atlantic Quarterly* 117, no. 3 (2018): 551–66.

———. *Animacies: Biopolitics, Racial Mattering, and Queer Affect.* Durham, NC: Duke University Press, 2012.

Chen, Tina. *Double Agency: Acts of Impersonation in Asian American Literature and Culture.* Stanford, CA: Stanford University Press, 2005.

Cheng, Anne A. *Ornamentalism.* New York: Oxford University Press, 2019.

Cheng, Cindy I-Fen. *Citizens of Asian America: Democracy and Race during the Cold War.* New York: New York University Press, 2013.

Cheung, Floyd. "Anxious and Ambivalent Representations: Nineteenth-Century Images of Chinese American Men." *Journal of American Culture* 30, no. 3 (2007): 293–309.

Chiu, Monica. *Filthy Fictions: Asian American Literature by Women.* Walnut Creek, CA: AltaMira Press, 2004.

Chong, Sylvia S. H. "Orientalism." In *Keywords for Asian American Studies,* edited by Cathy J. Schlund-Vials, Linda Trinh Võ, and K. Scott Wong, 182–85. New York: New York University Press, 2015.

Cintron, Ralph. "Democracy and Its Limitations." In *The Public Work of Rhetoric: Citizen-Scholars and Civic Engagement,* edited by John M. Ackerman and David J. Coogan, 98–116. Columbia: University of South Carolina Press, 2010.

Cisneros, Josue D. *The Border Crossed Us: Rhetorics of Borders, Citizenship, and Latina/o Identity.* Tuscaloosa: The University of Alabama Press, 2014.

Clary-Lemon, Jennifer. "'We're Not Ethnic, We're Irish!': Oral Histories and the Discursive Construction of Immigrant Identity." *Discourse & Society* 21, no. 1 (2010): 5–25.

Cohn, Victor. "Chinese Food Jinx Is Identified." *Washington Post,* July 14, 1968, A3.

Conley, Donovan, and Justin Eckstein, eds. *Cookery: Food Rhetorics and Social Production.* Tuscaloosa: The University of Alabama Press, 2020.

Cooks, Leda. "You Are What You (Don't) Eat? Food, Identity, and Resistance." *Text and Performance Quarterly* 29, no. 1 (2009): 94–110.

Cooley, Thomas M. "Ho Ah Kow v. Matthew Nuan." *Am. L. Reg.* 27, no. 11, 1879, 676–89.

Councilor, KC. "Feeding the Body Politic: Metaphors of Digestion in Progressive Era US Immigration Discourse." *Communication and Critical/Cultural Studies* 14, no. 2 (2017): 139–57.

Crawford, Robert. "Health as a Meaningful Social Practice." *Health* 10, no. 4 (2006): 401–20.

Creswell, John W. *Qualitative Inquiry and Research Design.* Lincoln: University of Nebraska, 2013.

Currarino, Rosanne. "'Meat vs. Rice': The Idea of Manly Labor and Anti-Chinese Hysteria in Nineteenth-Century America." *Men and Masculinities* 9, no. 4 (2007): 476–90.

D'Angelo, Frank. "The Evolution of the Analytic Topoi: A Speculative Inquiry." In *Essays on Classical Rhetoric and Modern Discourse,* edited by Robert Conners, Lisa Ede, and Andrea Lunsford, 50–68. Carbondale: Southern Illinois University Press, 1984.

Darling-Hammond, Sean, et al. "After 'The China Virus' Went Viral: Racially Charged Coronavirus Coverage and Trends in Bias Against Asian Americans." *Health Education & Behavior* 47, no. 6 (2020): 870–79.

Darrach, Amanda. "The New Coronavirus and Racist Tropes." *Columbia Journalism Review*, February 25, 2020. Accessed on September 1, 2020. https://www.cjr.org/analysis/covid-19-racism-china.php.

Davis, Nancy E. *The Chinese Lady: Afong Moy in Early America*. New York: Oxford University Press, 2019.

Day, Henry N. "The Chinese Migration." *New Englander and Yale Review* 29, no. 110 (1870): 1–23.

Day, Iyko. *Alien Capital: Asian Racialization and the Logic of Settler Colonial Capitalism*. Durham, NC: Duke University Press, 2016.

De Genova, Nicholas. "The 'War on Terror' as Racial Crisis: Homeland Security, Obama, and Racial (Trans)Formations." In *Race Formation in the Twenty-First Century*, edited by Daniel Martinez HoSang, Oneka LaBennett, and Laura Pulido, 246–75. Berkeley: University of California Press, 2019.

DeLaurier, Gregory F. "Thailand 1970." *Peace Review: War and Remembrance* 8, no. 2 (1996): 231–36.

Derkatch, Colleen. "The Self-Generating Language of Wellness and Natural Health." *Rhetoric of Health & Medicine* 1, no. 1–2 (2018): 132–60.

Dolmage, Jay. "Metis, Mêtis, Mestiza, Medusa: Rhetorical Bodies across Rhetorical Traditions." *Rhetoric Review* 28, no. 1 (2009): 1–28.

Douglas, Mary. *Purity and Danger: An Analysis of the Concepts of Pollution and Taboo*. London: Routledge, 1966.

DuPuis, E. Melanie. *Dangerous Digestion: The Politics of American Dietary Advice*. Berkeley: University of California Press, 2015.

Eckstein, Justin, and Anna M. Young. "wastED Rhetoric." *Communication and Critical/Cultural Studies* 15, no. 4 (2018): 274–91.

Eguchi, Shinsuke, and Godfried Asante. "Disidentifications Revisited: Queer(y)ing Intercultural Communication Theory." *Communication Theory* 26, no. 2 (2016): 171–89.

Eisner, Will. *Last Day in Vietnam: A Memory*. Milwaukee, WI: Dark Horse Comics, 2000.

Elias, Megan. "The Palate of Power: Americans, Food and the Philippines after the Spanish-American War." *Material Culture* 46, no. 1 (2014): 44–57.

Eng, David L. *Racial Castration: Managing Masculinity in Asian America*. Durham, NC: Duke University Press, 2001.

Eng, David L., and Shinhee Han. *Racial Melancholia, Racial Dissociation: On the Social and Psychic Lives of Asian Americans*. Durham, NC: Duke University Press, 2019.

Fegan, MacKenzie. "We Don't Need a White Wellness Savior to 'Fix' Chinese Food." *Vice*, April 10, 2019, 11:30 a.m. Accessed July 20, 2019. https://www.vice.com/en/article/3k38p9/lucky-lees-clean-and-healthy-chinese-food-is-not-needed.

Flores, Lisa A. *Deportable and Disposable: Public Rhetoric and the Making of the "Illegal" Immigrant*. University Park: Pennsylvania State University Press, 2020.

Florini, Sarah. *Beyond Hashtags: Racial Politics and Black Digital Networks*. New York: New York University Press, 2019.

Foucault, Michel. *The Archaeology of Knowledge*. New York: Pantheon Books, 1972.

———. *Power/Knowledge: Selected Interviews and Other Writings, 1972–1977*. Edited by Colin Gordon. New York: Pantheon Books, 1980.

"Fried Rice." *Ugly Delicious*, season 1, episode 7. Directed by Eddie Schmidt. Netflix, 2018.

Frye, Joshua, and Michael Bruner, eds. *The Rhetoric of Food: Discourse, Materiality, and Power*. New York: Routledge, 2012.

Fung, Eileen Chia-Ching. "Teaching Food and Foodways in Asian American Literature and Popular Culture: Special Issue." *Asian American Literature: Discourse & Pedagogies* 2 (2011): i–iii.

Gabaccia, Donna R. *We Are What We Eat: Ethnic Food and the Making of Americans.* Cambridge, MA: Harvard University Press, 1998.

Goehring, Charles, Valerie Renegar, and Laura Puhl. "'Abusive Furniture': Visual Metonymy and the Hungarian Stop Violence against Women Campaign." *Women's Studies in Communication* 40, no. 4 (2017): 440–57.

Goldthwaite, Melissa A., ed. *Food, Feminisms, Rhetorics.* Carbondale: Southern Illinois University Press, 2017.

Gompers, Samuel. "What Does Labor Want?" International Labor Congress, August 28, 1893, Chicago, Illinois.

Gompers, Samuel, and Herman Gutstadt. "Some Reasons for Chinese Exclusion. Meat vs. Rice. American Manhood against Asiatic Coolieism. Which Shall Survive?" The American Federation of Labor, 1901.

Gregg, Melissa, and Greg Seigworth. *The Affect Theory Reader.* Edited by Melissa Gregg and Greg Seigworth. Durham, NC: Duke University Press, 2010.

Halle, Randall. *Queer Social Philosophy: Critical Readings from Kant to Adorno.* Champaign: University of Illinois Press, 2004.

Halloran, Vivian N. *The Immigrant Kitchen: Food, Ethnicity, and Diaspora.* Columbus: The Ohio State University Press, 2016.

Haspel, Arielle. "Best Tips for Ordering in and Eating out at Restaurants." *Be Well with Arielle* (blog), April 23, 2014. http://www.bewellwitharielle.com/be-well/tips-eating-restaurants.

———. "Food Trends: What Diet Is Right for My Body?" *Be Well with Arielle* (blog), March 9, 2018. http://www.bewellwitharielle.com/be-well/food-trends-whats-hot-whats-not.

———. "Just Another Wellness Wednesday (Tamari)," *Be Well with Arielle* (blog), September 7, 2011. http://www.bewellwitharielle.com/snack-2/just-another-wellness-wednesday-tamari.

Hannis, Grant. "A Comparative Analysis of Nineteenth-Century Californian and New Zealand Newspaper Representations of Chinese Gold Miners." *Journal of American-East Asian Relations* 18 (2011): 248–73.

Harding, T. Swann. "Diet and Disease." *The Scientific Monthly* 26, no. 2 (1928): 150–57.

Hattori, Tomo, and Stuart Ching. "Reexamining the Between-Worlds Trope in Cross-Cultural Composition Studies." In *Representations: Doing Asian American Rhetoric,* edited by LuMing Mao and Morris Young, 41–61. Logan: Utah State University Press, 2008.

Hayot, Eric. *The Hypothetical Mandarin: Sympathy, Modernity, and Chinese Pain.* New York: Oxford University Press, 2009.

Hawhee, Debra. *Bodily Arts: Rhetoric and Athletics in Ancient Greece.* Austin: University of Texas Press, 2005.

Henderson, Alex. "Inside the 'Soy Boy' Conspiracy Theory: It Combines Misogyny and the Warped World of Pseudoscience." *Salon,* November 14, 2018. Accessed September 12, 2020. https://www.salon.com/2018/11/14/the-soy-boy-conspiracy-theory-alt-right-thinks-left-wing-has-it-out-for-them-with-soybeans_partner/.

Ho, Jennifer. "Acting Asian American, Eating Asian American: The Politics of Race and Food in Don Lee's *Wrack and Ruin.*" In *Eating Asian America: A Food Studies Reader,* edited by Robert Ji-Song Ku, Martin F. Manalansan, and Anita Mannur, 303–22. New York: New York University Press, 2013.

Holland, Sharon Patricia. *The Erotic Life of Racism.* Durham, NC: Duke University Press, 2012.

Hong, Cathy P. *Minor Feelings: An Asian American Reckoning.* New York: One World, 2020.

hooks, bell. "Eating the Other: Desire and Resistance." In *Black Looks: Race and Representation*, 21–39. Boston: South End Press, 1992.

"Horror Video of Woman Eating Bat in China." *The Morning Bulletin*, January 24, 2020. https://www.themorningbulletin.com.au/news/horror-video-of-woman-eating-bat-in-china/3928105/.

Houdek, Matthew. "Racial Sedimentation and the Common Sense of Racialized Violence: The Case of Black Church Burnings." *The Quarterly Journal of Speech* 104, no. 3 (2018): 279–306.

Johnson, Jenell. "'A Man's Mouth Is His Castle': The Midcentury Fluoridation Controversy and the Visceral Public." *The Quarterly Journal of Speech* 102, no. 1 (2016): 1–20.

Johnstone, Henry W., Jr. "Rhetoric as a Wedge: A Reformulation." *Rhetoric Society Quarterly* 20, no. 4 (1990): 333–38.

Kang, Laura H. Y. *Compositional Subjects: Enfiguring Asian/American Women*. Durham, NC: Duke University Press, 2002.

Kelly, Casey R. *Food Television and Otherness in the Age of Globalization*. Lanham, MD: Rowman and Littlefield, 2017.

Kennerly, Michele. "Getting Carried Away: How Rhetorical Transport Gets Judgment Going." *Rhetoric Society Quarterly* 40, no. 3 (2010): 269–91.

Khanna, Neetu. *The Visceral Logics of Decolonization*. Durham, NC: Duke University Press, 2020.

Kim, Claire Jean. "The Racial Triangulation of Asian Americans." *Politics & Society* 27, no. 1 (1999): 105–38.

Kimmel, Michael S. *The History of Men: Essays on the History of American and British Masculinities*. Ithaca: State University of New York Press, 2005.

King, Claire S. "Hitching Wagons to Stars: Celebrity, Metonymy, Hegemony, and the Case of Will Smith." *Communication and Critical/Cultural Studies* 14, no. 1 (2017): 83–102.

Kjær, Katrine M. "Detoxing Feels Good: Dieting and Affect in 22Days Nutrition and Goop Detoxes." *Feminist Media Studies* 19, no. 5 (2019): 702–16.

Kleiman, Carol. "Chinese Food Make You Crazy? MSG Is No. 1 Suspect." *The Chicago Tribune*, October 29, 1979, 1.

Kochhar, Rakesh, and Anthony Cilluffo. "Income Inequality in the U.S. Is Rising Most Rapidly among Asians." Pew Research Center, July 12, 2018.

Ku, Robert J. *Dubious Gastronomy: The Cultural Politics of Eating Asian in the USA*. Honolulu: University of Hawaii Press, 2013.

Ku, Robert Ji-Song, Martin F. Manalansan IV, and Anita Mannur, eds. *Eating Asian America: A Food Studies Reader*. New York: New York University Press, 2013.

Kubrick, Stanley, dir. *Full Metal Jacket*. Warner Bros., 1987.

Kwok, Ho M. "Chinese-Restaurant Syndrome." *The New England Journal of Medicine*, April 4, 1968, 796.

Lacy, Michael G., and Kent A. Ono. *Critical Rhetorics of Race*. New York: New York University Press, 2011.

Lee, Erika. "The Chinese Exclusion Example: Race, Immigration, and American Gatekeeping, 1882–1924." *Journal of American Ethnic History* 21, no. 3 (2002): 36–62.

Lee, Jerry Won. *The Politics of Translingualism: After Englishes*. New York: Routledge, 2017.

Lee, Robert G. *Orientals: Asian Americans in Popular Culture*. Philadelphia: Temple University Press, 1999.

Leighton, Caroline C. *Life at Puget Sound with Sketches of Travel Washington Territory, British Columbia, Oregon, and California 1865–1881*. New York: Lee and Shepard, 1884.

LeMesurier, Jennifer L. "Race as Supplement: Surfaces and Crevices of the Asian Feminine Body." *Quarterly Journal of Speech* 108, no. 3 (2022): 251–70.

———. "Somatic Metaphors: Embodied Recognition of Rhetorical Opportunities." *Rhetoric Review* 33, no. 4 (2014): 362–80.

———. "Uptaking Race: Genre, MSG, and Chinese Dinner." *Poroi* 12, no. 2 (2017): 1–23.

Leong, Karen J. *The China Mystique: Pearl S. Buck, Anna May Wong, Mayling Soong, and the Transformation of American Orientalism.* Berkeley: University of California Press, 2005.

———. "'A Distinct and Antagonistic Race': Constructions of Chinese Manhood in the Exclusionist Debates, 1869–1878." In *Race and Immigration in the United States: New Histories,* edited by Paul Spickard, 112–30. New York: Routledge, 2001.

Liu, Haiming. *From Canton Restaurant to Panda Express.* New Brunswick, NJ: Rutgers University Press, 2015.

Lopez, Lori K. *Asian American Media Activism: Fighting for Cultural Citizenship.* New York: New York University Press, 2016.

Lowe, Lisa. *Immigrant Acts: On Asian American Cultural Politics.* Durham, NC: Duke University Press, 1996.

@luckyleesnyc. "The other day we received some negative comments on an Instagram post. Some of your reactions made it clear to us that there are cultural sensitivities related to our Lucky Lee's concept . . ." Instagram, April 19, 2019. https://www.instagram.com/p/BwCk8aqnWsV/.

Lyon, Arabella. *Deliberative Acts: Democracy, Rhetoric, and Rights.* University Park: Pennsylvania State University Press, 2013.

Malatino, Hil. *Queer Embodiment: Monstrosity, Medical Violence, and Intersex Experience.* Lincoln: University of Nebraska Press, 2019.

Manning, Erin. *Politics of Touch: Sense, Movement, Sovereignty.* Minneapolis: University of Minnesota Press, 2006.

Mannur, Anita. *Culinary Fictions: Food in South Asian Diasporic Culture.* Philadelphia: Temple University Press, 2010.

———. "Model Minority Can Cook: Fusion Cuisine in Asian America." In *East Main Street: Asian American Popular Culture,* edited by Dave Shilpa, 72–94. New York: New York University Press, 2005.

Mao, LuMing, and Morris Young. *Representations: Doing Asian American Rhetoric.* Logan: Utah State University Press, 2008.

Massumi, Brian. *Parables for the Virtual: Movement, Affect, Sensation.* Durham, NC: Duke University Press, 2002.

———. *The Power at the End of the Economy.* Durham, NC: Duke University Press, 2015.

McGee, Michael C. "Text, Context, and the Fragmentation of Contemporary Culture." *Western Journal of Speech Communication* 54, no. 3 (1990): 274–89.

McKerrow, Raymie. Foreword to *The Rhetoric of Food: Discourse, Materiality, and Power,* xi–xiv. Edited by Joshua Frye and Michael Bruner. New York: Routledge, 2012.

Meade, Edwin. "The Chinese Question." Paper presented at the annual meeting of the Social Science Association of America, Saratoga, NY, September 7, 1877.

Mink, Gwendolyn. *Old Labor and New Immigrants in American Political Development: Union, Party, and State, 1875–1920.* Ithaca, NY: Cornell University Press, 1986.

Moon, Krystyn. *Yellowface: Creating the Chinese in American Popular Music and Performance, 1850s–1920s.* New Brunswick, NJ: Rutgers, 2005.

Morabito, Greg. "Racist 'Dirty Chinese Restaurant' Game Will Not Be Released." *Eater*, October 5, 2017, 3:02 p.m. https://www.eater.com/2017/10/5/16431268/racist-dirty-chinese-restaurant-game-cancelled.

Morris, Charles E., III. "Sunder the Children: Abraham Lincoln's Queer Rhetorical Pedagogy," *The Quarterly Journal of Speech* 99, no. 4 (2013): 395–422.

Mosby, Ian. "'That Won-Ton Soup Headache': The Chinese Restaurant Syndrome, MSG and the Making of American Food, 1968–1980." *Social History of Medicine: The Journal of the Society for the Social History of Medicine* 22, no. 1 (2009): 133–51.

Nakayama, Thomas K., and Robert L. Krizek. "Whiteness: A Strategic Rhetoric." *The Quarterly Journal of Speech* 81, no. 3 (1995): 291–309.

Ngai, Sianne. *Ugly Feelings.* Cambridge, MA: Harvard University Press, 2005.

O'Gorman, Ned. "Aristotle's *Phantasia* in the 'Rhetoric': *Lexis,* Appearance, and the Epideictic Function of Discourse." *Philosophy & Rhetoric* 38, no. 1 (2005): 16–40.

O'Keefe, Victoria M., et al. "Seemingly Harmless Racial Communications Are Not so Harmless: Racial Microaggressions Lead to Suicidal Ideation by Way of Depression Symptoms." *Suicide & Life-Threatening Behavior* 45, no. 5 (2015): 567–76.

Okihiro, Gary. "Perilous Frontiers." In *Yellow Peril: An Archive of Anti-Asian Fear,* edited by John Kuo Wei Tchen and Dylan Yeats, 195–99. Brooklyn, NY: Verso, 2014.

Olson, Christa J. "Performing Embodiable Topoi: Strategic Indigeneity and the Incorporation of Ecuadorian National Identity." *The Quarterly Journal of Speech* 96, no. 3 (2010): 300–323.

Ong, Anthony D., et al. "Racial Microaggressions and Daily Well-Being among Asian Americans." *Journal of Counseling Psychology* 60, no. 2 (2013): 188–99.

Ore, Ersula J. *Lynching: Violence, Rhetoric, and American Identity.* Jackson: University Press of Mississippi, 2019.

Orquiza, René A. D. *Taste of Control: Food and the Filipino Colonial Mentality under American Rule.* New Brunswick, NJ: Rutgers University Press, 2020.

Otterman, Sharon. "A White Restaurateur Advertised 'Clean' Chinese Food. Chinese-Americans Had Something to Say About It." *New York Times,* April 12, 2019. https://www.nytimes.com/2019/04/12/nyregion/lucky-lees-nyc-chinese-food.html.

Ou, Hsin-yun. "Chinese Ethnicity and the American Heroic Artisan in Henry Grimm's 'The Chinese Must Go' (1879)." *Comparative Drama* 44, no. 1 (2010): 63–84.

Oum, Young Rae. "Authenticity and Representation: Cuisines and Identities in Korean-American Diaspora." *Postcolonial Studies* 8, no. 1 (2005): 109–25.

Paddock, Richard C., and Dera M. Sijabat. "Where Bats Are Still on the Menu, if No Longer the Best Seller." *New York Times,* May 15, 2020.

Padoongpatt, Mark. *Flavors of Empire: Food and the Making of Thai America.* Oakland: University of California Press, 2017.

Palumbo-Liu, David. *Asian/American: Historical Crossings of a Racial Frontier.* Stanford, CA: Stanford University Press, 1999.

Panagia, Davide. *The Political Life of Sensation.* Durham, NC: Duke University Press, 2009.

Petersen, William. "Success Story, Japanese-American Style." *New York Times,* January 9, 1966.

Pham, Minh-Ha T. "Racial Plagiarism and Fashion." *QED: A Journal in GLBTQ Worldmaking* 4, no. 3 (2017): 67–80.

Pham, Vincent N. "Our Foreign President Barack Obama: The Racial Logics of Birther Discourses." *Journal of International and Intercultural Communication* 8, no. 2 (2015): 86–107.

Pham, Vincent, and Kent Ono. "'Artful Bigotry and Kitsch': A Study of Stereotype, Mimicry, and Satire in Asian American T-Shirt Rhetoric." In *Representations: Doing Asian American*

Rhetoric, edited by LuMing Mao and Morris Young, 175–97. Logan: Utah State University Press, 2008.

Prendergast, Catherine. "Asians: The Present Absence in 'Crash.'" *College English* 69, no. 4 (2007): 347–48.

Prestigiacomo, Amanda. "New York Times Labels Salad Racist. SALAD." *The Daily Wire*, April 17, 2017. https://www.dailywire.com/news/new-york-times-labels-salad-racist-salad-amanda-prestigiacomo.

Puar, Jasbir K. *Terrorist Assemblages: Homonationalism in Queer Times*. Durham, NC: Duke University Press, 2017.

Rao, Sonia. "Bon Appétit Video Stars Leave the Test Kitchen Series Due to Alleged Racial Discrimination." *Washington Post*, August 7, 2020. https://www.washingtonpost.com/news/voraciously/wp/2020/08/06/three-bon-appetit-video-stars-leave-the-test-kitchen-series-due-to-alleged-racial-discrimination/.

Ratcliffe, Krista. *Rhetorical Listening: Identification, Gender, Whiteness*. Carbondale: Southern Illinois University Press, 2005.

Ray, Krishnendu. *The Ethnic Restaurateur*. London: Bloomsbury, 2016.

Raymundo, Emily. "Beauty Regimens, Beauty Regimes: Korean Beauty on YouTube." In *Fashion and Beauty in the Time of Asia*, edited by S. Heijin Lee, Christina H. Moon, and Thuy Linh Nguyen Tu, 103–26. New York: New York University Press, 2019.

Real Time with Bill Maher. HBO, April 10, 2020.

Rice, Jenny E. "Unframing Models of Public Distribution: From Rhetorical Situation to Rhetorical Ecologies." *Rhetoric Society Quarterly* 35, no. 4 (2005): 5–24.

Rodney, Alexandra. "Pathogenic or Health-Promoting? How Food Is Framed in Healthy Living Media for Women." *Social Science & Medicine* 213 (2018): 37–44.

Roediger, David. *How Race Survived U.S. History: From Settlement and Slavery to the Eclipse of Post-Racialism*. Brooklyn, NY: Verso, 2019.

Roy, Parama. *Alimentary Tracts: Appetites, Aversions, and the Postcolonial*. Durham, NC: Duke University Press, 2010.

Russia Today. "Video of Woman Eating Whole Bat Emerges as Scientists Link Coronavirus to the Flying Mammals." *YouTube*, January 25, 2020. https://www.youtube.com/watch?v=oZsFHu-AaGQ.

Said, Edward. *Orientalism*. New York: Vintage Books. 1979.

Sand, Jordan. "A Short History of MSG: Good Science, Bad Science, and Taste Cultures." *Gastronomica* 5, no. 4 (2005): 38–49.

Sekimoto, Sachi. "Race and the Senses: Toward Articulating the Sensory Apparatus of Race." *Critical Philosophy of Race* 6, no. 1 (2018): 82–100.

Shah, Nayan. *Contagious Divides: Epidemics and Race in San Francisco's Chinatown*. Berkeley: University of California Press, 2001.

Shesgreen, Deidre. "'A Loaded Gun': Wet Markets, Wildlife Trafficking Pose Threat for the Next Pandemic." *USA Today*, May 16, 2020, 6:00 a.m., updated May 19, 2020, 1:04 p.m.

Shimizu, Celine P. "The Bind of Representation: Performing and Consuming Hypersexuality in 'Miss Saigon.'" *Theatre Journal* 57, no. 2 (2005): 247–65.

Shome, Raka. *Diana and Beyond: White Femininity, National Identity, and Contemporary Media Culture*. Urbana: University of Illinois Press, 2014.

Smith, Mark M. *How Race Is Made: Slavery, Segregation, and the Senses*. Chapel Hill: University of North Carolina Press, 2006.

Specht, Joshua. *Red Meat Republic: A Hoof-to-Table History of How Beef Changed America.* Princeton, NJ: Princeton University Press, 2019.

Stewart, Kathleen. *Ordinary Affects.* Durham, NC: Duke University Press, 2007.

Stoffels, Sven (@svenstoffels). "Corona CHingChan does a 'lil dance for us. #corona #covid19 #chinesevirus #chinavirus." Twitter, April 22, 2020. pic.twitter.com/OHnSKshHtE.

——. "When will China take legal and financial responsibility for a health crisis and viral pandemic that ravaged nations worldwide? #cancelchina." Twitter, May 12, 2020. https://twitter.com/svenstoffels/status/1260193107175510022.

"Stop AAPI Hate Report." Stop AAPI Hate, May 13, 2020. https://stopaapihate.org/3-month-report/.

Swanton, Dan. "Sorting Bodies: Race, Affect, and Everyday Multiculture in a Mill Town in Northern England." *Environment and Planning A: Economy and Space* 42, no. 10 (2010): 2332–50.

Tchen, John K. W. *New York before Chinatown: Orientalism and the Shaping of American Culture, 1776–1882.* Baltimore: Johns Hopkins University Press, 1999.

Tchen, John K. W., and Dylan Yeats. *Yellow Peril: An Archive of Anti-Asian Fear.* Brooklyn, NY: Verso, 2014.

The Hill (@thehill). "Sen. John Cornyn: 'China is to blame because the culture where people eat bats & snakes & dogs & things like that, these viruses are transmitted from the animal to the people and that's why China has been the source of a lot of these viruses like SARS, like MERS, the Swine Flu.'" Twitter, March 18, 2020. https://twitter.com/thehill/status/1240364608390606850?s=20.

"They Blamed Me Because I Am Asian." Stop AAPI Hate, September 17, 2020. https://stopaapihate.org/youth-campaign-report/.

Tippen, Carrie H. *Inventing Authenticity: How Cookbook Writers Redefine Southern Identity.* Fayetteville: University of Arkansas Press, 2018.

Tompkins, Kyla W. *Racial Indigestion: Eating Bodies in the 19th Century.* New York: New York University Press, 2012.

Tsui, Bonnie. "Why Is Asian Salad Still on the Menu?" *New York Times,* April 27, 2017. https://www.nytimes.com/2017/04/27/opinion/sunday/why-is-asian-salad-still-on-the-menu.html.

Tsui, Bonnie, et al. "Why We Can't Talk about Race in Food." *Civil Eats,* June 27, 2017. https://civileats.com/2017/06/27/why-we-cant-talk-about-race-in-food/.

Tuder, Stefanie. "New NYC Chinese Restaurant Draws Swift Backlash to Racist Language." *Eater,* April 9, 2019, 10:13 a.m., updated April 9, 2019, 12:20 p.m. https://ny.eater.com/2019/4/9/18301861/lucky-lees-chinese-open-controversy-nyc.

Twain, Mark. *Roughing It.* Orinda, CA: SeaWolf Press, 2018.

Twitty, Michael. *The Cooking Gene: A Journey through African American Culinary History in the Old South.* New York: Harper Collins Publishers, 2017.

Vats, Anjali. "(Dis)owning Bikram: Decolonizing Vernacular and Dewesternizing Restructuring in the Yoga Wars." *Communication and Critical/Cultural Studies* 13, no. 4 (2016): 325–45.

Venugopal, Anun. "Demonstrators, Elected Officials Rally after Surge in Anti-Asian Hate and Violence." *The Gothamist,* February 28, 2021. https://gothamist.com/news/demonstrators-elected-officials-rally-after-surge-anti-asian-hate-and-violence.

Wallach, Jennifer J., and Lindsey R. Swindall. *American Appetites: A Documentary Reader.* Fayetteville: University of Arkansas Press, 2014.

Walzer, Christian, and Aili Kang. "Abolish Asia's 'Wet Markets,' Where Pandemics Breed." *Wall Street Journal,* Eastern edition, January 28, 2020.

Warnick, Barbara. "Two Systems of Invention: The Topics in the 'Rhetoric' and 'The New Rhetoric.'" In *Rereading Aristotle's Rhetoric*, edited by Alan G. Gross and Arthur E. Walzer, 107–29. Carbondale: Southern Illinois University Press, 2000.

Washington, Myra. *Blasian Invasion: Racial Mixing in the Celebrity Industrial Complex.* Jackson: University Press of Mississippi, 2017.

Watson, Paul. "The Truth about Soy Boys." *YouTube,* November 16, 2017. https://www.youtube.com/watch?v=FTSvLKY7HEk.

Watts, Eric K. "Postracial Fantasies, Blackness, and Zombies." *Communication and Critical/Cultural Studies* 14, no. 4 (2017): 317–33.

Wei, William. *Asians in Colorado: A History of Persecution and Perseverance in the Centennial State.* Seattle: University of Washington Press, 2016.

Whole30 (@whole30). "NEW WHOLE30 RULE: MSG is perfectly acceptable during your Whole30." Twitter, December 20, 2021, 11:41 a.m., https://twitter.com/whole30/status/1472970382042828807.

Williams, Rhaisa K. "Toward a Theorization of Black Maternal Grief as Analytic." *Transforming Anthropology* 24, no. 1 (2016): 17–30.

Wilson, Mark. "Andrew Zimmern: 'Bizarre Foods' Had a Cultural Insensitivity Problem." *Fast Company,* November 20, 2018. https://www.fastcompany.com/video/andrew-zimmern-on-bizarre-foods-there-was-a-lot-of-cultural-insensitivity/Po6VvIdR.

Winderman, Emily. "Anger's Volumes: Rhetorics of Amplification and Aggregation in #MeToo." *Women's Studies in Communication* 42, no. 3 (2019): 327–46.

Woan, Sunny. "White Sexual Imperialism: A Theory of Asian Feminist Jurisprudence." *Washington and Lee Journal of Civil Rights and Social Justice* 14, no. 2 (2008): 275–301.

World Health Organization (@WHO). "DO—talk about the new #coronavirus disease (#COVID19). DON'T—attach locations or ethnicity to the disease, this is not a 'Wuhan Virus,' 'Chinese Virus' or 'Asian Virus.' The official name for the disease was deliberately chosen to avoid stigmatization." Twitter, March 2, 2020. https://twitter.com/WHO/status/1234604060420005888.

Wu, Frank H. *Yellow: Race in America beyond Black and White.* New York: Basic Books, 2002.

Xu, Wenying. *Eating Identities: Reading Food in Asian American Literature.* Honolulu: University of Hawai'i Press, 2008.

Yam, Shui-Yin S. *Inconvenient Strangers: Transnational Subjects and the Politics of Citizenship.* Columbus: Ohio State University Press, 2019.

Yang, Misti. "Phantastic, Impressive Rhetoric." *Philosophy & Rhetoric* 54, no. 4 (2021): 374–96.

Yang, Zoe. "As Coronavirus Panic Spreads, I Went in Search of Wuhan's Defining Dish." *Bon Appetit,* February 26, 2020. https://www.bonappetit.com/story/coronavirus-panic.

Yoon, K. Hyoejin. "Learning Asian American Affect." In *Representations: Doing Asian American Rhetoric,* edited by LuMing Mao and Morris Young, 293–322. Logan: Utah State University Press, 2008.

Zhang, Qian F., and Zi Pan. "The Transformation of Urban Vegetable Retail in China: Wet Markets, Supermarkets and Informal Markets in Shanghai." *Journal of Contemporary Asia* 43, no. 3 (2013): 497–518.

Zhu, Annah, and George Zhu. "Understanding China's Wildlife Markets: Trade and Tradition in an Age of Pandemic." *World Development* 136 (2020): 1–4.

Zia, Helen. *Asian American Dreams: The Emergence of an American People.* New York: Farrar, Straus and Giroux, 2000.

INDEX

affect: bodies and, 17; dominance and, 15; gut orientations and, 127–28; habituated, 17; social bonding power of, 85; viscerality and, 81

affect theory, 15n46, 85

Ahmed, Sara, 2, 4, 18, 68

alt-right, 3–4

Alvarez, Steven, 111n34

American Dream, 47, 119

American exceptionalism, 111

anime, xiv

appetite, 12, 28, 58–64, 85

Asante, Godfried, 102–3

Asian: as "model minority," xiii, 19–20, 49, 54, 99–101, 116–20; "right" sort of, 116–20; as term, xiv, xv

Asian American: as "next in line" to be white, 19–20, 109–10; as privileged, 110; as term, xiv, xv, xvn10

Asian female sexuality, 69–74, 71 fig. 5, 73 fig. 6

Asian male sexuality, 66

Asian masculinity, 24, 36–40

"Asian salad," 100–101, 105–18, 131–33. *See also* Tsui, Bonnie

Asianness, 5, 8, 40, 49; as foreignness, 6; gender stereotypes of, 100; post-racial, 18–21, 105–16; rhetorical stance of, 101

assimilation, 19–20, 36–37, 41–43, 47, 88, 100–102, 106, 112

authenticity, 7–8, 86, 101, 104, 108–12, 111n34, 112, 131–32

Bailey, Cathryn, 36

bats, 52, 57, 61–62, 66–69, 66n49, 67 fig. 4, 69n55, 128

Beach, Hannah, 58n22

beef, xii, 43–44

Berkhofer, Robert, 116

Bhabha, Homi, 31

biases: gut orientations and, 2; proximity and, 7; taste and, 79; in wellness discourse, 80, 96

Big Brother (television show), 3

Biltekoff, Charlotte, 9

birthplace, 54–55

INTERSECTIONAL RHETORICS

KARMA R. CHÁVEZ, SERIES EDITOR

This series takes as its starting point the position that intersectionality offers important insights to the field of rhetoric—including that to enhance what we understand as rhetorical practice, we must diversify the types of rhetors, arguments, frameworks, and forms under analysis. Intersection works on two levels for the series: (1) reflecting the series' privileging of intersectional perspectives and analytical frames while also (2) emphasizing rhetoric's intersection with related fields, disciplines, and research areas.